THE MOTHER TIME LETTERS

A JOURNEY INTO SOUL TIME

THE MOTHER TIME LETTERS

A JOURNEY INTO SOUL TIME

CAROLYN W. TOBEN

PUBLISHED BY
TIMBERLAKE EARTH SANCTUARY PRESS
2020

Cover Art
"Great Solstice Moon"
Copyright © 2009 by Mary Southard, CSJ
www.MarySouthardArt.org

Book design by Scott Davis

Published by
Timberlake Earth Sanctuary Press
Whitsett, North Carolina, U.S.A.
www.timberlakeearthsanctuary.com
books@timberlakeearthsanctuary.com

Printed in the United States

ISBN 978-0-9883928-3-0

For "the family of humankind walking toward the Light."
—Thomas Berry

Contents

PREFACE

IT IS APRIL, "the cruelest month of the year," said the poet T. S. Eliot, who could have been describing the entire world in April 2020, as we stand at a cruel still point; stopped, ground down to a complete halt by a deadly virus that seems bent on human extinction. No one is exempt from its brutal, relentless, militant march forward. Prime ministers, celebrities, rich, poor, the seemingly healthy, the already sickly . . . in this still point, all are vulnerable.

Closures are everywhere . . . schools, companies, stores, churches, synagogues, parks. Only grocery stores, hospitals, essential services, and funeral homes remain open. We are told to "self-quarantine" and "social distance" ourselves, and those who do venture forth wear homemade face masks and carry hand sanitizers. Our conversations focus on hand-washing, antibacterial soaps, disinfecting wipes, and the absence of toilet paper on store shelves.

And it is the same all over the world . . . in every country, city, town, village, home, apartment, tent. We struggle to understand the magnitude of this pandemic and how to cope with the daily death toll. Only budding dogwood trees, the songs of cardinals and chickadees, and the sweet, earthy smells of spring offer any semblance of normalcy and comfort.

This, then, is the context for the publication of this book that I have been sheltering for over four decades. I never intended to share its spiritual contents . . . until now—now that the deep suffering of this time is creating an urgency for its disclosure.

In these pages, you will find a life-transforming story of a spiritual presence who appeared in my life one afternoon many years ago. I was flying home from a trip to help resolve a family crisis that had not ended well. On the plane, in deep emotional distress, I reached into my carry-on bag and removed my journal to write down my feelings. For some unknown reason, I drew a squiggly line down the center of a page and began writing on the righthand side. When I came to the end of the page, I lifted my pen to continue on the lefthand side, and was startled to hear the following words in my mind:

> My dear One,
> You are seeing nothing as it is now. You are seeing only the past. From now on, I will be guiding you into soul time where you will learn to see differently . . .
>
> Lovingly,
> Mother Time

To my astonishment, as I heard these words and wrote them down, I felt inwardly strengthened and reassured. I spent the rest of the flight repeating them over and over.

In the days and months that followed, the family crisis resolved itself without my help, but my own inner difficulties deepened.

I consulted Mother Time again and again by writing letters to her and receiving wisdom from the letters she wrote back to me. Along with compassionate words, she revealed her spiritual presence and a deep soul friendship through the years that followed.

Mother Time took me on a journey into soul time in which she taught me to go beyond the limited personality level to the deeper level of the heart. In that secret space, I learned that within each of us there is a holy place of the soul, an inner Light and softly speaking Voice to which we may continually return by re-membering this truth inwardly in soul time. Each moment devoted to this sanctuary by seeking the inner self through reflection, meditation, prayer, and contemplation not only moves us out of linear time but also strengthens our ability to meet great difficul-ties by allowing us to hear interior messages of Love that can finally become our own.

Mother Time taught me that we all have a natural soul intelli-gence that directs us to a sense of the sacred that can only be found through introspection. She offered life-changing lessons by sug-gesting "stopping places" in my daily life where she taught me to see anew in holy moments of soul time where I discovered that relationships are the primary context of existence and the earth and all its creations constitute one sacred community. At this age and stage of my life, my prayer is that her letters can offer guid-ance and hope to other seekers.

Mother Time was concerned with the healing needs of both the individual and the collective, explaining that we live in a period of time in which the evolutionary process is accelerating on every level in an ever-expanding universe.

Each of us is an individual soul within the World Soul, and every soul's advance or regression affects the whole. In the words of cultural historian Thomas Berry, "We are organized to grow on."

Mother Time's letters awaken us to a deeper consciousness of our innate loving nature as well as our negative qualities that need to be transformed. She speaks not only to our psychological growth but also to our spiritual hunger for reunion with the Divine. Her active presence in every moment of soul time brings us into a new awareness of the Divine Feminine that longs to join soul to Spirit, true feelings to analyses, intuition to reason, subjectivity to objectivity, and, most importantly, affirms the One Love that can finally overcome human egoism.

Mother Time's deep vision offers us hope for our own healing and for the whole of creation. Through her, if we listen closely, we can not only hear echoes of ancient spiritual perspectives that have come down through the ages, but also gather new understanding desperately needed in this critical moment of transition on Earth to which we have been assigned.

Within these letters are pathways to remedy past time and "grow on." I offer her words to you in loving gratitude.

Carolyn Toben
Fall 2020

THE MOTHER TIME LETTERS

My dear One,

I am here in answer to your prayers for help. In truth, I have been silently traveling with you on an inner, parallel path throughout your life . . . as light in the darkness of disordered thought, as hope in the rubble of changing form, as courage in the face of overwhelming obstacles. You have experienced me as life at the bedside of death, as warmth in the coldness of grief, as health in the depths of illness, as a sentinel during times of temptation, as protection in the perils of danger, as enduring Love in the midst of guilt and fear. Know that I will always be present with you for as long as you need me.

You write that you feel like you are standing with great uncertainty "at a threshold between two worlds." You know that you cannot return to your old ways, but you cannot see a way to go forward—even though you intuitively know that change must occur, and you are willing to reach out for inner guidance.

Once you are willing to reach out, help can be offered. Now there is much for you to hear that you were not ready to hear before. The time was not right. Everything in the universe moves in a particular order, though it may not always *seem* to be true.

For a "threshold" to emerge in one's life, a certain degree of energy must precede it. In your case, that has been true, has it not, with the very difficult circumstances you describe? And . . . you are living in a historic time in which the intensity of negative energy is causing great suffering and injustice in the world.

You hear the great cries . . . from human and non-human alike. Your own cry is for the loss of "something sacred," as you put it, "that can give your life meaning at this time." You write that you feel "something is awakening inside you," but you don't know how to make sense of it and instead feel fear and anxiety.

I must tell you that the chaos of your time is a necessary stage in human evolution, and the appearance of thresholds is a warning that it is time for the old to fall away so a new mode of existence can come into being. You and your world are in transition. Humans can no longer live on this earth in the same destructive ways. Humankind must evolve or face extinction. The current conditions of separation, fragmentation, brutality, and neglect have brought on global disease. A critical stage has been reached.

You are a microcosm of the macrocosm with your deep feelings of personal separation and fragmentation, which finally bring me to speak through these letters. For the sufferings of your time are both personal and universal—one and the same. They cannot be separated.

I have accepted the assignment of guiding you along two pathways of personal transformation. First, replacing the negative mental patterns that have undermined the human story. Second, the recognition of *soul-spirit knowledge* with its intuitive understanding and new ways of seeing. Both must be included for the evolution of consciousness to go forward. As the brilliant scientist Albert Einstein once said, "The problems of this time cannot be resolved at the same level at which they were created."

The universe is calling you and all of humanity to evolve to a new level of soul consciousness in this very critical time. Your personal story is part of the larger story of evolution. Everyone is being called to participate in the re-creation of that Great Story by becoming increasingly conscious of their outer and inner lives . . . The above and below must now be brought together.

My work is to guide you over the threshold of your present-day awareness at the level of your personality to the larger memory of your original soul-spirit connection. Humans have more profound inner capacities than they realize, and I am directed to guide you in this interior development.

Lovingly,
Mother Time

My dear One,

My guidance is meant to be a source of light for your current dark and chaotic subconscious mind. Breathe deeply and listen carefully to the message I bring you: "Something new is happening. A new vision, a new energy, a new sacred story is coming into being that all are a part of but of which few are aware. In the darkness of this time, a vast transformation is occurring in the depths of human consciousness—a transformation that can lead to the recovery of the soul-spirit, the earth, and a sense of the sacred that has been nearly lost for centuries.

Your science has confirmed that the universe is expanding, and each recovering soul is experiencing this expansion now. You are in strange and unfamiliar *inner* terrain at this time, but I can tell you that this is a time of great transition on Earth that can bring about a new level of understanding that is imperative for the evolution of human history. Hear the words of the beloved spiritual teacher Thomas Berry, "We are being changed. We are being transformed to see everything in its proper proportion. We are being driven down to the heart with its radical interior tendencies."

The new sacred story is about a transition into ways of seeing with the heart, a transformation coming from the future that can lead to new pathways of evolution for both the personal and the universal, which are inextricably interwoven. It is a transition that will take a full willingness to accept the deepest reality of humanity's spiritual nature and soul identity.

Remember that . . . "In the beginning," 13.8 billion years ago, the immense sacred story began with the emergence of the physical universe and the vast cosmic-human-process created by Divine Love as a physical and spiritual reality. This One sacred unity was meant to develop through the ages. The purpose of the universe was to bring life and Love to every form on Earth. Each individual soul was created as an expression of the Divine and given unique qualities unlike any other. In the words of Ecclesiastes, "eternity was set in the heart," so the pure, indwelling Holy Spirit of Divine Love would be forever embedded in the soul. This holy gift was to be remembered throughout one's life, moment by moment, as an eternal Light that nothing could extinguish. It was a sacred bond, an inseparable connection from the heart of Divine Love to the heart of each soul as the basis of all relationships on Earth.

But through the ages, a very different story began to take place as individual souls forgot their deep inner connection with the Holy Spirit and the sacred bond that brought Love into every relationship on Earth. Instead, people began to believe that what God created could be improved upon by their own minds and that they could create themselves and everything around them. Tragic consequences followed: the holiness of creation was shattered into fragments, as the whole purpose of time without the dimension of an inner soul time became a linear march toward material progress, efficiency, achievement, acquisition, power, and simulated worlds.

This ascendence of linear time has created an imbalance that is harming you and endangering your planet. To begin to understand the current conditions of your life, you must come to know the differences between linear time and soul time.

In linear time, the external taskmaster receives unquestioned homage. In soul time, internal time springs from the life force within.

Linear time defines time as tempo. Soul time defines it as endurance, continuity, rhythm, as in the phases of the moon and the turning of the seasons.

In linear time, "passing time" hurtles forward at an ever-accelerating pace, whereas in soul time, the NOW moment contains all the fullness necessary to meet every need. Each concentrated moment may be seen as containing all: past, present, and future. Each full moment of soul time may also be seen as new.

Linear time acquires, grasps, clings. Soul time heals, creates, releases. In linear time, priorities attach to tasks. In soul time, priorities attach to relationships. Linear time separates humankind into individual egos that are distinct from one another, Earth, and Spirit. Everything is organized around differences—parts are dissected, analyzed, and judgments prevail. In soul time, the womb of creation gives birth to a knowledge of connectedness that links all parts to the whole.

In linear time, separateness and a sense of the impersonal lead to soul diminishment, whereas in soul time, the ego exchanges powerlessness for a deeply inner personal identity as soul reunites with Spirit, Earth, and others.

In linear time, life as a physical experience sees only through the eyes of the body. In soul time, life as a spiritual experience sees through the eyes of the heart.

In the accelerated tempo of linear time, moments of meaning are lost. In soul time, moments of meaning are recovered, revealing the soul in its infinite depth and complexity.

In the tempo of linear time, time compresses and contracts, denying entry to transformation. In soul time, time expands, thoughts reverse, perceptions heal, and transformation can occur through forgiveness.

In the compression of linear time, the whole of creation cannot be remembered. In the expansion of soul time, the soul hears its voice and flows into a natural relationship with it. In linear time, the creating activities of feeling, sensing, imagining are omitted. In soul time, they are restored.

Horizontal linear time defines distinct beginnings and endings. Circular soul time recognizes the ceaseless movement of the eternal spiral from deep within that rises, falls, and renews . . .

Linear time defines time mathematically. Soul time redefines it in every moment that the soul brings spiritual consciousness to it. As Ecclesiastes says, "a time to break down and a time to build up . . . a time to weep and a time to laugh; a time to mourn and a time to dance . . ."

Linear time focuses on the outer, the visible, the known. Soul time focuses on the inner, the invisible, the unknown.

In order for human evolution to go forward, linear time and soul time must be reconciled so that balance may be restored by bringing these opposites together. Now, in this time of severe crisis on Earth, the two must come together in a synthesis that integrates mind and heart.

A new sacred story—both personal and collective—must emerge through the recovery of the spiritual dimensions of soul time. This process, which may require unlearning and relearning, will take great patience and perseverance as each soul-spirit takes up this great work and merges with others who are committed to the same sacred service.

Your own "awakening," as you describe it, is directly connected to the larger story which you have unconsciously accepted as your reality until now. You will be creating a new story from within yourself as you step across the threshold with a multitude of others who are traveling a parallel path. They come from every walk of life, every wisdom tradition, age, color, gender, religion, and culture. They are poets, artists, scientists, mystics, clergy, scholars, and teachers. "A family of humankind walking toward the Light."

Lovingly,
Mother Time

My dear One,

You are already making progress in your soul development as you ask questions. As it is said, "Large questions lead a civilization forward."

In response to your continuing threshold questions about soul and Spirit, I must say that these questions are best answered through your *own lived experiences* of the spiritual life. In this way, one's inner convictions grow, and the answers each discovers may be offered up to create new foundational understanding for those who follow. But in this moment, here is what I can offer you.

If you will return to the origin story of creation, you will remember that "in the beginning," each soul was created in an individualized image of Divine Love and forever connected to God through the presence of the Holy Spirit. This was the same for all souls on Earth. Deep within each individual was the purity of the soul—the Light that continues without interruption—and the Spirit was the connection between the soul and the Divine.

Each soul was entrusted with the care and development of its own pure Light, which had to be *understood* and *practiced* in order to remember its Creator and the thoughts of God. If this learning failed to take place, the ego could arise with a very different thought system that would erase the memory of the soul's purity. The individual would then carry an emptiness, a "home-sickness," you might say, through its entire life, for it forgot the holiness-wholeness originally given it by God. The individual still carried the unique gifts given it at birth by the Divine, but the egoism that developed within its personality caused great trouble, leading to the kind of crisis you are now experiencing. In this crisis, one must do the soul-searching you are being led to do now by examining your belief systems and following only those thoughts that lead you back to Love and rejecting those that lead to ego, for only Love can overcome human egoism.

In this often painful process, you must remember that you have been given the Spirit connecting the soul to God. According to the distinguished religious anthropologist Mircea Eliade, this is an actual element in human consciousness that is forever seeking expression.

You have been awakened by this Spirit, whose presence guides you as you seek to discern the difference between those thought systems that come from linear time and those that come from soul time, and the consequences that follow from each. The Spirit recognizes the original purity of your soul and works unceasingly to restore it to awareness as the deepest innermost eternal part connected to God. It acknowledges the soul as the meeting place between the human and the Divine and longs to lead the soul to its fulfillment, knowing that each soul is absolutely unique and can bring into the world what no other can as an expression of the Divine.

I hope these words have brought greater clarity and an understanding that through the centuries, others have also struggled mightily with these same deep concerns. You must know you are never alone. In the words of author Diarmuid Ó Murchú, "Spirituality is an innate quality of human life and existence. It is something we are born with." It is a powerful force that wants to be revealed, and you are now in its loving embrace.

Lovingly,
Mother Time

My dear One,

Today, you might say, is the beginning of a new beginning where you make the conscious choice to "go another way" from a life grown stagnant from outmoded thoughts that constantly challenge your newly evolving consciousness of imagination, Spirit, creativity, and Love. Linear time with its fixed concepts of relationships, outmoded patterns of interactions, neglect of the natural world, and norms of corruption, greed, and subservience does not serve the human evolutionary process of your time. You are now determined to find or create another world in this world. As I have explained to you, your soul longings will lead you to others who also yearn to create a shared future with the heart-mind as their compass.

To begin your journey, cross the threshold and come into the pure memory of your Divine connection, remembering that "you are as God created you." Breathe deeply and thankfully as you go forward in your "ordinary" life with a new awareness that calls you to see—not only outwardly but also *inwardly*—as you go through your daily life experiences. As you do so, you will have many opportunities to make new decisions that align with your changing values. You will also find what Thomas Berry said is true: "Intuition is like a tendril connected to the heart of the universe" and is another way of knowing.

I will guide you gently into the realm of soul time through your daily experiences and your relationships with yourself and others, the Divine, and Earth. Each soul-spirit's recovery has a very particular curriculum that unfolds as each life experience is examined, and the habitual thinking of linear time gives way to soul time awareness. The true definition of "idea" is to see. Above all else, seek to "see" with your heart-mind that the Divine is immanent as well as transcendent.

The process is often exceedingly slow and may take you through an ongoing organic cycle of decay and death of the old, fertilization and gestation of the new, and the sprouting of rebirth as the seeds of soul time take root and slowly begin to produce "first the blade and then the ear." Love will work its holy purpose as soul time blossoms into visibility, and balance is restored within linear time.

I will help you STOP in openings of linear time to allow quiet moments of soul time to reveal Love's presence. In these momentary pauses, you will discover secret meeting places between the physical world and the spiritual world and participate in their long overdue reunion. These moments will become communions as you recover within them the Spirit, the sacred, the earth. As you learn to embrace these communions, your soul will be strengthened, and, in turn, you will strengthen the whole of creation as you remember that you are never alone in the effects of what you think, say, or do.

Lovingly,
Mother Time

My dear One,

You are now joining the great force-field of those companions on the evolutionary pathway walking toward the Light. The purpose of these letters is to guide you along the circular spiral journey into soul time. You already have expressed soul longings that are like bread crumbs strewn before you to follow, but I will remind you that the larger vision you carry is that of remembering that you came from Love and are on a journey to recover Love as you share it with others. When the great violinist Yehudi Menuhin was asked how to play great music, he replied, "Keep your eye on a distant star." Remembering Love amidst the obstacles that your soul encounters is a similar holy endeavor . . .

I will assist you as you move beyond the narrow, time-boundedness of linear time into the spaciousness of soul time, which is the reality of your true existence. It will be a movement, not away from Earth, but ever more deeply into it. You will gradually come to see the inner living qualities of all others as you experience the larger reality of soul time and a sense of reunion with Earth, Spirit, human and non-human, and the Divine. We will repeat these thoughts often, for a good teacher knows that repetition strengthens.

You will not be satisfied with less, for as the soul seeks to recover its original ancient connection to Spirit through daily practices, the journey will increasingly develop and deepen. Each soul is assigned highly specific tasks that are revealed along the way. Each soul encounters countless obstacles that must be overcome. I will help you reduce the clutter of your subconscious mind so that the Light of your Spirit can shine through you to bring soul time into linear time.

If this all sounds difficult, remember: Soul consciousness is a wellspring of faith, hope, and purpose that cannot be shattered.

Lovingly,
Mother Time

My dear One,

Continuing with our communication on the personality and the soul from your recent questions . . .

First of all, we know that the ego—that personality shell we have built around ourselves—surfaces whenever we find ourselves responding to another person out of a sense of superiority or inferiority, which is a product of the conditioned past of linear time. There is no blame. No one escapes the necessity of creating a self that can survive life's difficult circumstances. Each soul adapts roles in linear time that have prescribed behaviors and artificial goals. Often one feels caged in as the personality falls victim to its own falsely created temperament. This can lead to a crisis that, in the words of Vincent Van Gogh, "seeks a way to make the cages vanish."

This is your struggle now and is a familiar one for many others who long to liberate themselves. What you do not realize is that the human soul also holds the key for your release.

With the scientific understanding of the expanding universe, there is an equivalent spiritual realization that human expansion is also enlarging on every level, including the inner level of the pure soul's connection to the Divine.

Each individual soul carries both the inner purity of God along with whatever obscures it. On your journey, you will discover others who are seeking ways to free themselves from the layers of life's accumulated obstacles in order to return to the purity of Divine Love, their true source.

This is actually the soul's deepest longing, and you will hear different versions of this as you join the journey. The stories may be different, but the longing is always the same. Everyone is a prisoner until they find the solution within themselves to open the prison door. Deep down, everyone on the soul-spirit journey is seeking the holiness that will transform their lives.

Love is that holiness. Love, my dear, is an inner presence to all things and emanates from the same Source that created everything from the tiniest creature to the human soul. It is the Oneness, actually, of Love that can unlock the prison door and release the small imprisoned self into the larger Universal Self.

And so, as your journey progresses, you will have many opportunities to become aware of Love, not only around you but within you. You will receive help from many others you will meet, and you will help them in return. Giving and receiving Love will show you the way.

Lovingly,
Mother Time

My dear One,

The mystery of time is within. You have asked to enter into that mystery more deeply, and it is my task to assist you so that you, in turn, can assist others who come this way. You are beginning to understand that as you halt more and more frequently to absorb the NOW moments of your life, your soul forces are strengthening, and you are better able to meet daily obstacles with increased balance and equanimity.

You ask why this is so, and I will explain it to you. Your conditioned mind believes itself to be in linear time, either bolting ahead into a future that is never there or falling back into a past that you made up out of bits and scraps of perceptions from another stage of development. This much you have become aware of, and your willingness to recognize this error and then STOP and re-direct your thoughts has led you to new inner growth. In truth, it is these stopping places in life that lead to soul growth, for the stopping places are the NOW moments—the only time in which changes can be made.

In your "stopping places," you are discovering that your whole sense of time is shifting from one that is narrow and linear to one that is huge and circular. It might be said that instead of existing in a small dark cabin lit only by a tiny candle, you are more frequently living in the luminous and spacious temple of soul time where you can behold a bright, distant star.

When you find yourself feeling the narrowness or diminishment that comes from falling back into linear time, STOP and remember to let go, and soul time will be there, as it always is . . .

Lovingly,
Mother Time

My dear One,

The function of time, as I have told you before, is for the healing of attitudes. It is for finding new perspectives, "new altitudes," a way in which to see all things anew. It is a rising above the antipathies of the personality level to see all others without judgment of any kind. When one judges, one separates oneself from others and is therefore in linear time, whereas letting go of judgment releases one into soul time.

It is a common human error to form fixed opinions without remembering the possibility of going beyond them to discover the larger inner soul space in which Love blesses all.

Lovingly,
Mother Time

It is a common human error to form fixed opinions without re

My dear One,

Today you are feeling a need to connect deeply with others. You have asked how this might be accomplished, and already you are receiving increased warmth from the people around you—a smile, the sound of a favorite song, and the smell of roses . . . There can be the anticipation of yet more to come this day if you are willing to make a prayerful request of Spirit.

You are aware of the endless artificial distinctions that individuals unconsciously make to keep themselves from experiencing the heart connections they long for—differences in age, economic status, cultural backgrounds, fear of intimacy, fear of dependency. Even a self-conscious spirituality can be a barrier to communication with others.

It is not generally understood that the search for reunion with Spirit, and the need to be in deep relationship with others, is one and the same.

Lovingly,
Mother Time

My dear One,

I am encouraged to read that you have discovered that identifying your own set of shadow qualities is having a remarkable effect on your life. You write that you are "somehow" experiencing new levels of physical energy as a result of our soul work together. That by "stopping" and redirecting your thoughts, you seem to be gaining new mental clarity too.

This is most heartening to me as I see you "growing on" in your soul development, as you know I like to say. All of Heaven rejoices as you learn to release the negative fixations that have unconsciously held you in chains for so long. Now that you are willing to release them, instead of expressing them as they make their way through the door of your subconscious mind, you use the skills from your meditative practice to simply notice and allow them to pass harmlessly through your heart-mind. As one of the dear souls I once accompanied liked to say, "I try to give everyone a safe passage through my mind."

As you grow on, the negatives, not receiving the attention they long for, grow weaker and weaker, and eventually drop off . . . And as you continue to become more and more aware, you will begin to notice that instead of reacting too quickly from the ego, which likes to jump in with an opinion in any situation, you are listening for the "second voice" of Spirit to provide a wiser and more nuanced response. Soon you will learn to become more and more mindful in all that you do and say as your discernment deepens.

It just takes time—soul time.

Lovingly,
Mother Time

My dear One,

Do not be afraid to let yourself down into the cold waters of grief and mourning. Your love for the one who has died is greatly honored. As teacher and soul friend, she recognized your deepest Self, allowing you to participate in the miracle of personal transformation in which one discovers new possibilities for one's life.

Standing tall in her own life like a wick in a candle, she lit the way for countless others by showing them how to see themselves as she saw them. She fully accepted the conditions of her own life but allowed the difficulties she faced to release greater powers. When her days were over, she left the earth like a flower that has come to full bloom.

Grieve now, my child. The deep gratitude of your loving memories will assist your loved one as she makes her transition to a greater life. As you sink down into the cold waters, you will rediscover the warm spring below that will return you to present time and renew you with a very real knowledge that there is no death. For only the body "dies." The soul remains in Timelessness.

You are being comforted now by those who are with you in soul time.

Lovingly,
Mother Time

My dear One,

You are experiencing the deep contraction of the soul as it shrivels to a pinpoint in response to a verbal attack from a loved one. You say your hearts seem to have grown cold toward one another. Let it be for now. Be willing to enter into the pain of misunderstanding between those connected by family ties. Bear the blows in the privacy of your heart and return them not. Let go of your defenses. Always remember that an attack from another is a cry for help. Take your pain inside where it can be healed and continue to send your love to this family member.

A family is a group of souls who come together on Earth to learn to love one another. A family is the most significant context in which to learn communion and soul growth. Forgiveness can be practiced as the members of a family become more conscious of the diversity among them and increasingly learn acceptance and appreciation of that diversity.

That is the inner work required of a group of souls who have incarnated as a family. When there is a rupture, such as the one you are now experiencing, it is the responsibility of the soul who has the greater awareness at the time to set forgiveness in motion.

You are that soul in this case, and your task in this NOW moment is to take your pain into the huge temple of soul time where it will be absorbed. You will then be able to send loving forgiveness and compassion to your family member for whatever pain or fear prompted the attack. And when the time is right, and you will intuitively know when that is, you can initiate repair of the relationship.

Remember, everything you say, do, or even think affects the whole of creation.

Lovingly,
Mother Time

My dear One,

In the night, you hear a bird's song and the dripping water trickling down the window after a recent rain. Against this moment, your heart aches for a loved one in a spiritual crisis. You affirm the inner wisdom of his soul as well as the wisdom of soul time. You know that each soul's development brings with it the pain of awakening. You experience this in your own life, yet you resist a loved one's similar journey into darkness in an effort to shield him from suffering. Originally the word suffering meant to "undergo a passage," and your loved one is going through such a dark passage now.

Go into the sacred space of soul time, and in your imagination, light a candle to hold in the darkness to guide your loved one's way through his passage.

And continue to trust the gentleness of the bird song and the trickling water of the night.

Lovingly,
Mother Time

My dear One,

This evening you are experiencing feelings of dread and fear in anticipation of an encounter with a dear one who has become a stranger to you. You doubt that the temple of soul time is large enough and strong enough to bear the outcome, and you have asked to see this situation differently.

Let your imagination move you from your motel room with its humming air conditioner, gaping closet doors, and darkened TV set across the room. Move instead to a picture of the whole motel against the stormy winter sky. Then allow your mind to enlarge the scene to include the whole state, the nation, the world, and the planet.

Now allow your mind to gather together all the feelings of those on Earth who are estranged from their loved ones tonight. Hold the enormity of this pain that goes beyond tears. Feel your own pain connecting with the suffering of others as your heart opens with deep compassion. In this sacred moment of soul time, feel yourself being held and healed.

As you return in your imagination to the motel room, your dread and fears withdraw. You see that the size and strength of the temple will hold all that is needed now.

Lovingly,
Mother Time

My dear One,

You long to understand how forgiveness can come at this moment when your mind, as you put it, is in "a frozen condition."

Look out the window of the airplane and see below the corresponding frozen condition of the earth with its covering of ice and snow. The miles of white held in a clear blue haze create a scene of stillness. As a mother marveling at her sleeping child, see the delicate veins and arteries of rivers and lakes temporarily silent.

Now, imagine your sleeping child beginning to stir under the covers and reaching upwards to find your gentle warmth awaiting her. In immediate response to your embrace, the sun pours out its rays through an opening in the blue haze.

May this image warm and thaw your mind and heart.

Lovingly,
Mother Time

My dear One,

Waves of fear and defensiveness rise up within you as you approach a family crisis. You feel the dreaded tightening around your heart and in your neck. Neither fight nor flight will do. Breathe—breathe—breathe. Activate your alternative inner system of soul time.

Know that a moment of reconciliation is about to occur. Allow the image of healing Love in the form of powerful ocean waves to rise up. As they gain force and strength, the waves of fear and defensiveness dissolve harmlessly on the shore.

Your inner peace gladly returns.

Lovingly,
Mother Time

My dear One,

As you incorrectly label a situation in your mind and then react to your own label, let me offer you another picture. The word "label" refers to a narrow strip or shred of material used to identify something. Its current meaning comes from the strip of parchment that encircled a document and bore a seal.

Imagine breaking that seal and opening the document. Once the label is removed, you find these words inside: "Release and let go."

> Lovingly,
> Mother Time

❧

My dear One,

Do not be afraid to descend once again into the darkness, for there you will also find Spirit. Enter now into the heavy shadows of grief and pain, knowing that you are not alone. Enter into your fears for your loved ones. I share in your feelings of powerlessness as you stand by and see them suffer.

Your hands are empty; you have nothing more to give—no more encouragement, no more thoughts, no more gifts, no more comfort. There is nothing left to *do* as you see your loved ones seemingly disappear into the cold realm of analytical judgment and abstract thought. Here in this darkness, you touch the garments of other mothers, who, through the centuries, have experienced the suffering of estrangement from loved ones. Know that in this dark realm, there is kindness for you.

In your grief and anger toward a culture that does not honor warmth, compassion, and love, there is kindness for you. Know that you have nourished the seed of Spirit within your loved ones. Trust that those seeds will open when the time is right. Remember the ceaseless movement of all nature: birth, death, decay, fertilization, gestation, rebirth.

In this moment, look out your window at the tight buds of the rhododendron covered with ice. They are protected by hard outer casings that contain them. They will bloom again when spring comes.

Trust the life process in all things.

Lovingly,
Mother Time

❦

My dear One,

Pay attention to what you are feeling because there is a barrier that you must overcome to reach Love in soul time. You have attained it many times before, and although you have returned to fear, you know you *can* find Love again.

Every barrier contains an unforgiving element that is connected to the past of linear time. Is there something in a past relationship, perhaps with a parent or other family member, that needs healing? If so, recall that person in your memory and forgive them, for every relationship must be made whole.

It matters not whether they are in physical form. They are always present in Spirit, and they long for your forgiveness. They did the best they could with the awareness they had at the time. They were not aware of the infinite range of differences in human nature, and out of their unknowing, sought to conform you into their way of being instead of your own.

Forgive them. Hear them say to you now from that realm of higher understanding, "We did not know. We know now. We understand and send you our deepest love and appreciation for your life, your work, your healing. We thank you for all that you gave to us—all that you meant to us when we were on Earth. We love you dearly and bless you. Let the relationship between us be cleansed of old resentment, blame, and guilt, so that you are not reminded of it ever again. Remember only the Love that we intended for you."

Now, as the barrier dissolves, you return to Love in soul time.

Lovingly,
Mother Time

My dear One,

I will offer this help as you search for a new viewpoint in your struggle with emotions that are overwhelming you in an estranged relationship.

Stand, my dear, at the very point on the beach where the waves surge in and out. Draw a heart in the wet sand, and each time the waves wash it away, wait a moment, and draw it again . . .

And again . . .
And again . . .
And again . . .

Lovingly,
Mother Time

My dear One,

I call your attention to a truth you have forgotten. Out of the battle of the opposites in your nature, you can find a new synthesis, a new state of being, a new awareness that sees the holiness-wholeness of life.

If you project that battle outwardly on others instead of taking responsibility for it *within* yourself, your new awareness cannot grow. Thus, if you really want to expand and learn, you must not get bogged down in male-female issues. You must move beyond stereotypes to examine your own interior reactions within each context of your life. Otherwise, you will lapse further into the collective consciousness, which polarizes differences with its potential ruptures.

Your spiritual task is healing, not disjunction.

Lovingly,
Mother Time

My dear One,

You are suffering today with a certain grief that accompanies your realization of the loneliness that exists within each human soul. It has been truly said that no two people on Earth are exactly alike in anything except their loneliness. But I must tell you that it is that same loneliness and grief that keeps the search for Love alive.

The great error comes when the search leads to complete dependence on another human being, material possessions, or power, for the disappointments and disillusionments in these directions are inevitable. Enormous pain could be prevented on Earth if it was really understood that Love creates each individual like itself, and, therefore, each soul is an individualized representation of that Love. Do you *see* how the world could be re-imagined if this truth were realized? The task of each individual soul is to rediscover this truth and then extend it into every relationship, human and non-human.

When two souls work to realize this truth together, they experience the greater Divine Love given to them in the beginning that connects their hearts and dissolves their loneliness.

Lovingly,
Mother Time

My dear One,

As you struggle to find new perspectives in your relationships, turn to the natural world, and let your senses lead you to healing within soul time.

Become aware of the smell of the ocean as the waves swirl around the wet rocks and wash over your feet.

Become aware of the longings that wash over your soul like these relentless waves rolling in from the sea.

"Listen," says the tide.

"Listen," say the sea birds.

"Look outward and inward," cries the horizon. "There is always more."

Hear a seagull squeal in the sunshine.

See the pink granite rocks dappled with tiny green clover and mustard-yellow lichen.

Search out the deep. Dare to go down under the sea to the farthest point.

Let the natural world heal you.

Let the ebb and flow of relationships—now together, now apart, now upward, now downward—make themselves known to you.

Refuse to be fixed in any single definition of form. Let the fluid, ever-changing contours of relationship simply BE like this moment in soul time. You cannot do or change anything, any more than you can control the movement of the ocean, the rolling of the waves, the calling of the gulls. Relationships create an endless and uneven arc of attachment, detachment, harmony, discord, and reattachment . . .

Remember the aim is not always for resolution according to one's own expectations, but always for greater understanding.

Kneel, and give thanks for this sacred NOW moment.

Lovingly,
Mother Time

∽

My dear One,

Trust that somewhere in this moment and the ones that follow, you will find the miracle of transformation you are seeking.

You are presently aware of nothing but your worry and concern for a loved one. Your inner skies have darkened, your chest tightens with pain, and your aching head longs for sleep to escape your distress.

Yet, in this moment, I ask you to move your attention gently outward. Become aware of the sun coming through the east window, casting a square frame of light on the front of the armoire facing you. Watch that frame of light temporarily disappear as a cloud overshadows the sun, then reappear even more brightly as the cloud passes on. Allow that movement to bring you a slight sense of renewal.

Now become aware of the sun touching and blessing more of the room with its light as it rises still farther in the sky. Allow your thoughts to rise with it, trusting their natural tendency to do so.

Next, walk outside to follow the course of the sun as it moves upward. See the tall pear tree with its barren winter branches and notice how the sun creates long, finger-like shadows on the ground. Move your attention quietly inside that "outstretched hand" and stand there feeling its comfort and protection.

Now, walk into the woods and become aware that you are still accompanied by the sun, that you can move nowhere without its presence.

You cry out, "My loved one has a cancer," and the World Soul echoes back, "*My* loved one—Earth—has a cancer."

"Please help me," you plead, and you hear echoed back, "Please help me."

And the sun replies, "Only Love can help, a Love that expands, touches, and blesses . . .

Lovingly,
Mother Time

My dear One,

Everywhere you walk, birdsong accompanies you in a call and response. Different textures—a ripple, an extended line, a jagged sound—produce a rhythm of song woven through by the buzzing of zigzagging flies. Pink honeysuckle languishes over a fallen branch on your left. Tall grasses sway beyond the fence on your right. Gravel crunches beneath your feet. In the dim background, a mourning dove coos softly. A small plane passes by overhead.

As you walk down the hill into a small valley, you see the miracle of the mountain laurel in full bloom. The trees are blowing in the wind, casting dappled shadows on the path. As you reach out, the blossom of a mountain laurel seems to float into your open hand.

Your heart is heavy with sorrow in the midst of this beauty. Your thoughts assail you. Your left eye twitches. Your chest is heavy. All you can think of is that one of your adult children is suffering inwardly, and there is nothing you can do to help. Your wisdom tells you, "You must let go of your worry." You ask the question, "How can I let go of my concern?"

A woodpecker answers with a rat-a-tat-tat on a tree high above your head as if mindful of your pain. You realize that the fear you feel for the future of your loved one has led you into linear time. You have fallen deeply into old patterns of motherhood that are no longer appropriate. You cannot fix anything for your loved one today, as you did in an earlier stage of your development and his. Both of you have changed. Your relationship has changed. Yet, you are still linked by the same roles as in the past.

You must now change your inner picture to conform to the present moment. Your loving attention that tried to make all things right for your children when they were young must now be re-placed by the picture of a mother who lets go of all control and trusts the life process that comes out of her own experience. In truth, your old role must die so that your children can grow in their own unique ways.

You cannot give your loved ones any of your thoughts or ideas; they have their own. You cannot give them any comfort; others in their lives must comfort them now. Now, you must bless them and walk away, knowing that you have done all you can. You must set them free. You must not follow them into their dark-ness or into their Light. Everything must be relinquished except the love you will always hold for them throughout eternity.

Love, my dear, has been so narrowly interpreted and so badly distorted that the spiritual task of your time is to recover its true meaning. It has been interpreted as affection or desire for another person, thing, or event outside oneself. In that interpretation, it is about possessing something you do not have.

The truth is that Love—or God—created each soul for Itself and, therefore, there is nothing to acquire. Look at the natural world around you, which was created by the same Love that created you. It asks for nothing. It wishes to acquire nothing. It simply is . . . accepting all things as they are—the sunshine, rain, lightning, thunder, and darkness.

Be like the blossom of the mountain laurel you are holding in your hand—open, vulnerable, gentle, and unafraid—even as your thoughts try to pull you down into the shadow of death now flooding your heart with tears. See how the deep mental grooves of fear in which you are mired have been obliterated by that flood.

Now, start your walk uphill from the valley into the sunlight. You need not look back again.

Lovingly,
Mother Time

❦

My dear One,

You ask how to help a loved one who is suffering inwardly.

Imagine that you are able to focus your love with the same intensity and concentration that one is able to focus the rays of the sun through a magnifying glass. The heat from your loving pinpoint of Light can cause a circle of flame that overcomes the darkness with which you are struggling.

In such a manner, you are cooperating with the angelic forces of soul time already at work on her behalf.

Lovingly,
Mother Time

❦

My dear One,

Refuse to analyze the sensations you are now experiencing in your chest. Describe them instead as a pressure you feel building within accompanied by feelings of sadness for which there is no apparent cause. Go out into the spring evening and turn your attention to the tiniest sounds you can hear—beyond the barking of the dogs and the steady chorus of the tree frogs, beyond the settling-in sounds of the birds, beyond the call of the dove. Hear each fade softly away—the dogs padding away on soft feet, the noise of tree frogs subsiding, the birds plumping down for the night—each leaving behind faint echoes of their presence.

Into this space enters the fragrance of honeysuckle that surrounds and holds memories of a day rich in images of precious time spent with elderly friends who have come to visit the home that you and your family have created here. You have loved and blessed this land and every object in your dwelling place. Those who enter feel the presence of Spirit here. In this way, the world is transformed.

Your task is simply to let go and allow yourself to move ever more fully into soul time, trusting the continuous unfoldings of your life and work in an effortless way. Whenever you find yourself feeling stressed as you have today, STOP. Allow this holy space to surround and envelop you once again, and you will *know* that all is well.

Lovingly,
Mother Time

My dear One,

In the silence of the moment, you seek to understand the tools of forgiveness. You suffer tonight from a heart grown cold from painful interactions with loved ones.

Your attention is drawn to the hearth. There stands a set of iron utensils—a shovel, a poker, a small broom, and a scoop for the ashes. The image of the fireside tools reminds you that they are only useful when stirring up the fire *after* it is ignited or *after* the fire has gone out. Before the fire is built, the tools have no purpose. They simply wait on the hearth to perform their function. Only when the fire has been lit are they useful, and only *you* can light the fire.

The tools of forgiveness are *within* you, my dear. Blow on the coals of your heart to bring forth the warmth of your hearth.

Lovingly,
Mother Time

My dear One,

As you make your way carefully over the frozen snowbank by the lake, your mind goes to a family member who seems to be stalled in a phase of his life development.

Allow your attention to move to the seed pods of the sycamore tree, which have blown off and are now held lightly by the ice on the lake.

Remember that—
Warmth will return,
the lake will thaw,
the seed pods will crack open,
and new life will come forth.

Let go again, trust the process of life, and go back to your own . . .

Lovingly,
Mother Time

My dear One,

Within the pain and grief of your relationship with a loved one, you recall the rhythm of labor and the practices you have learned. Merge with the rhythm as the pain surges over you. Breathe into it; ride with it. STOP. It is gone but will return again. You are giving birth to an enlarged capacity for increased compassion and depth.

Here in the darkness and pain, you are not alone. On the inner level, the loving mid-wives of soul time are here to assist.

Lovingly,
Mother Time

My dear One,

At this moment, the woods beckon you with a message of compassion as you awaken to the grief for a loved one who has died and left a deep legacy of humor, courage, and perseverance in his final soul development period on Earth.

As you walk along the path through the tall trees, you see the sunrise in the distance. The white clouds are colored by faint pink and orange streaks. As the sun rises higher, the colors deepen as if in loving tribute.

Your heart fills with tenderness in knowing that this is the natural succession of life with Divine order at the head and heart of the processional.

Lovingly,
Mother Time

My dear One,

You realize that in each moment, you have what you need if you are willing to look out and see it.

Through the half-opened window of your hotel room in a large city, you only hear the squeal of tires, the rumble of garbage trucks, the banging of trash cans, horn honks, ambulance sirens, and the roar of a jet overhead. Inside your mind, you only hear the painful thoughts and hurt feelings from a failed communication with a loved one.

Allow the Love from soul time to absorb the hurt feelings. Open your window wide and look outside. See how much more you can comprehend when the bright sky reveals the entire city in all its diversity. Instead of your partial perception, look outward to see the whole picture of this NOW moment.

> Lovingly,
> Mother Time

My dear One,

The important thing is to refrain from jumping to conclusions as the conditioned mind of linear time would tempt you to do. Instead, allow space for a new future to enter. Resist the temptation to judge as if you fully know the current situation.

The truth is, you may not know the whole story. All you can say for sure is, "I do not know what anything is for." Be willing to give over to soul time your preconceptions and conjectures.

Just as it is true that there is always more that one can know about any material object, remember there is always more to know about *every situation.* Behind all external events, there is an inner weaving taking place in soul time. Consider the alternations of light and dark, finite and infinite, joy and sorrow. You only have to *watch,* and you *will see what soul time can teach you.*

Lovingly,
Mother Time

My dear One,

You are experiencing the inner pain of a difficult encounter with another from whom you felt a blow that hurt you at the deepest inner level. *Do nothing.* Simply pay attention to what is happening within you right now. You are being taught through your inner soul training that there is a purposefulness in all things, even though you cannot see it now. Do not analyze the situation. Make no decisions. Simply be with the pain, and trust that the transforming activity of Spirit is working within you.

Do not be afraid to retreat inwardly as animals often do when they experience a blow. At this moment, all you can truthfully say is, "I don't know what anything is for." For now, that is enough.

Sleep. I am watching over you.

Lovingly,
Mother Time

My dear One,

Today you awoke with less pain but with an inner frozen "place" that tells you there is more to go through before healing is complete. You asked the question, "What do I need to *see?*" and found that your present pain is connected to pain from the past.

For your tears to be released and your soul reunited with Spirit, you must forgive those in the past. One by one, you must mentally embrace and forgive every person who unconsciously caused you pain. Once you do, your frozen feelings will thaw, and peace will return.

Often it is true that in order to go forward in soul time, one must go backward. Always remember, your intention is to heal and create.

> Lovingly,
> Mother Time

My dear One,

You have awakened with continuing emotional pain from your abusive encounter with a colleague. You try to turn your attention outward to the India ink outlines of the pine trees and the miracle of the morning sun, but you are overwhelmingly conscious of your inner pain. Do not try to flee from it, but go about your tasks with it accompanying you. Watch inwardly for clarity or direction to come.

A slight shift prompts you to write to your colleague to describe your perceptions of the encounter, your feelings about it, and your decision to step aside from further interactions. Still, the pain persists, both in your stomach and your chest. Now you are tempted to simply sink into your negative feelings, allowing them to take you over completely. This you must resist, for the soul work here is to keep them from gaining ascendancy.

Again, remember the ever-present offerings of Spirit, and go on about your tasks and appointments, always watching for the transformational shift.

It takes great strength to stay with your feelings, my dear. You have now funded that strength by trusting them, and they will not abandon you.

Nor will we in soul time who are supporting your soul evolution.

Lovingly,
Mother Time

My dear One,

Can you begin to understand even slightly that you do far more to serve others by stopping in these moments and being still? Your willingness to be *present*—"before the *essence*," as the word truly means—is the greatest help you can offer those in need.

You must fight the temptation to problem-solve for others, for it is one of the most subtle forms of ego control. You can do nothing except be present for them. That is all, and that is ALL.

Dare to stay on your own path in soul time.

Lovingly,
Mother Time

My dear One,

Do you see how negative emotions cloud your lens for seeing the world clearly? When your thoughts are darkened by grievances of any kind, the world is darkened as well. You are completely responsible for *how* you see and *what* you see. So you must be about the work of purifying the conditioned mind of linear time. This is your primary task.

Stand tall like the pine trees reaching toward the light. Allow the sunlight to filter through you to banish the forms of guilt and fear that you uncover. When the interlopers realize you have discovered them, they will drop their feeble hold on you and disappear into the darkness.

With each small victory, the Light within grows brighter.

Lovingly,
Mother Time

My dear One,

Today you awoke without emotional pain but with physical pain in your head and upper body. The blow you sustained in your encounter with another has now worked its way from deep within your soul to your physical body and will soon be gone entirely. Negative thoughts still assail you but are beginning to lessen. As you pray for help to bring about complete healing, four images come to you. *Fire*, which offers to burn away the residue of negativity you are carrying. *Water*, which offers to wash away any lingering impurities. *Air*, which offers to lift you up with thermal wind under your wings so you can see your present situation from a higher perspective. *Earth,* which offers her most intimate communion to replace your mind's tendency to return again and again to your recent grievances.

The danger is that you will fall from one illusion, that of victim, into another, that of self-righteousness. The ego delights in seeing itself as either "less than" or "greater than." Your spiritual identity in soul time is neither of these; it simply *is,* just like the poplar tree you see standing outside your window.

Concentrate on it. Let its enduring qualities impress themselves on you. The poplar simply accepts all that comes its way as part of the life process.

Be like the poplar tree with its roots deeply embedded in the soil.

Lovingly,
Mother Time

My dear One,

Can you see that out of conflict, new awareness comes—and a cleansing of the inner dwelling place of Spirit? Your struggles against the darkness of your soul can bring you to greater faith and clarity than ever before. Rejoice that you can always trust the life process and the awareness of soul time to lead you out of the darkness.

In your recent bout with the darkness, you were required to go deeply into the often rocky layers of the soul, unearthing feelings brought on by old thought forms from linear time that have not yet been transformed. At each layer, like a meticulous archeologist, you brought them up, sifted through them, and examined them carefully, releasing tears and anger in the protecting presence of the natural world. Finally, at the darkest moment of encountering the deepest bedrock of pain, you found the joy that surpasses all understanding as your inner life released you from your suffering.

As it says in the Book of John, "You shall know the truth, and the truth shall set you free."

Lovingly,
Mother Time

My dear One,

By now, you realize that the inner "work" is about removing every obstacle from the full expression of the Spirit of Love within you.

In your recent negative encounter with a colleague, you have experienced deep feelings of woundedness, guilt, indifference, and, to a much lesser extent, anger. You still feel "blocked" and try to make a token effort at forgiving your attacker but find it insincere and empty. It is only human to try to move quickly past a difficult encounter, but there is still another lesson you must learn here.

I must tell you that in order to move past this present block, you must return to anger and welcome its lessons, for it has much to teach you. You have denied it for so long that you have trouble recognizing it, but anger knows you well. Listen carefully as it speaks to you:

"You have never paid attention to my needs. You have discounted and ignored me entirely for fear that I would cause you alienation or condemnation from others, which you could not bear. Yet, by denying me, you are now experiencing separation from your own heart. Own me, express me in constructive ways, and I will be your friend. Ignore me at your peril, for I will erupt and wreak havoc in your life and in the lives of others. For I am a force to be used to call attention to that which has been ignored and denied in your own life and in the lives of others of your time.

"I will come to your aid when you have been unjustly treated in any way. You will feel my presence in your body where I dwell. At those times, express me clearly without fear or guilt. Trust the moment you are in and always act out of your deepest feelings.

"I will also come to you when others in your path are unjustly treated. Again, I will demand that you pay attention to me, or I will do serious damage to your body. I will also accompany you as you encounter the radical ills of this time.

"You must learn to recognize, acknowledge, and express me. For too long, I have been excluded from your consciousness out of your ignorance that I, Anger, am a creative life force that has the power to heal as well as destroy. Use me to say *no* to all things that keep your soul from moving forward. Use me to deal effectively with what comes toward you that you know in your heart is not for you. Do not link me with fear, guilt, or self-righteousness, for then I will become destructive. Use me as a pure soul force, and I will show you new ways of Love."

Anger speaks truly, my dear. It is *time* to listen. The alchemy of transformation is speaking your truth.

Lovingly,
Mother Time

My dear One,

Today, as you sit beside the small creek after weeks of straining to gain a new standpoint on your painful encounter with a colleague, you simply allow yourself to weep in anguish over misunderstandings between people on Earth. To your surprise, in this moment, you discover that the pain has been eased.

Allowing the World Soul to express its anguish through you releases you to see that all souls have many of the same difficulties, and thus there is no need for forgiveness.

Compassion brings transformation and healing—"water to wine."

> Lovingly,
> Mother Time

My dear One,

It is early morning in the city, and the skies are gray outside your room. You hear the sound of two cars colliding, a siren screaming, the angry beeping of a falsetto horn, the squeaking of bus brakes as they come quickly to a halt.

In this moment, fear posing as anger dominates your consciousness—it takes bodily form as pressure in your chest, shallow breathing, fearful images forming in regard to the future of a dear loved one who is on his way to work at this hour.

Your fear extends beyond this room. It cannot be contained within the physical surroundings but moves from deep within your body and seeps out into the world, affecting others with its yellow-green toxicity. Reverse it now. Take it by the hand to the altar of Love in soul time. Let it be transformed so that it no longer hurts you or the world of which you are a part. See it turn to the healing color of clear, deep green.

Notice that outside your hotel room, the traffic seems to be moving easily now.

Lovingly,
Mother Time

❧

My dear One,

In this time of intense emotional crisis, you need do nothing more than STOP.

↪ Allow the space of soul time to serve you as a crucible for Love's healing power.

↪ Let the many forms of fear be dissolved within the crucible by the alchemy of Love.

↪ Stand quietly upright within the tension of opposites and contradictions that engulf you from all sides.

↪ Be actively present to the flame-like qualities of long-buried emotions as they leap up, die down, and re-ignite, always honoring the unconscious mind as it labors toward the Light of greater consciousness. Respect all vulnerabilities, including your own.

↪ Place no limitations on Love's power to heal and bless. Dare to ask for the highest good for all concerned.

↪ Let your constant prayer be for your words to come directly from your heart.

↪ Refrain from making any decisions or coming to any conclusions. Instead, observe the healing process as it unfolds this day.

෴ Be open to receiving the help emerging from your inner and outer worlds. Allow the sunshine to melt your grief. Allow the moon to cool and soothe the heat of anger.

෴ Remember always your oneness with your loved one. Each of you has a story, but the story of your relationship is larger than either story alone. It is the story of the great legacy of forgiveness. In the end, from the ashes, a new, stronger relationship will be forged through this transformational process from the heart of the Divine.

෴ Plant a garden. Sing a song. Give constant thanks.

Lovingly,
Mother Time

My dear One,

Tonight, keep being vulnerable, consciously allowing feelings long-buried to surface in order to be healed. Allow a large space for anger to be vented without taking on blame. As it comes toward you, STOP, and allow the force of your Love to reverse it completely. Trust that the power of Love in this situation is healing all involved. You are surrounded by Divine forces who support the transforming work you have undertaken. The angels of your loved ones are in close proximity, grateful for a place of entry.

Your friends, the moon and the stars, hover close by, the spring air allows your breathing to become even. You are inwardly still, knowing that all is unfolding in Divine order.

Lovingly,
Mother Time

My dear One,

You say you long to participate more fully in your relation-ships.

Then listen deeply for greater understanding when your loved ones speak. Listen with your whole being. Tip-toe softly behind the words that are spoken, not to intrude, but to Love ever more deeply into the heart of the other.

Lovingly,
Mother Time

My dear One,

Hear . . .

The Word,
the utterance
that can be heard, be seen—

Hear it, see it now as you enter into the mystery of Love, the mystery of the deep connection with all things. Within the jagged lightning of crisis, that deep connection is revealed.

In the shatteredness, the Real is exposed.
Love and humankind are one.
Nothing Real can be threatened.
Nothing unreal exists.
Whom Love hath joined nothing can put asunder.
Be-hold.

Lovingly,
Mother Time

My dear One,

Over and over again, I must help you *remember* the moment you are in now. Today, in your willingness to reach out and support others, you became overwhelmed by their needs and found yourself buried under an avalanche of problems.

Now is the time to STOP and disengage. STOP and come into the stillness of the moment in which the only sound you hear is the hum of a distant truck on a highway and the soft rotation of the ceiling fan above. Become aware of the way the movement of the fan generates shadows across the ceiling and throws waves of light across the surface of the family pictures on the table below.

In the context of this moment, experience soul time—the past that brought you here, the future that will come out of it. Let them meet here in this holy instant of healing, of wholeness.

Lovingly,
Mother Time

My dear One,

You are moving ever more deeply into new dimensions of trust on your journey. You *see* that the continual activity of Spirit in soul time is always at work within you to clarify and purify your soul.

As you awaken to this presence through the process of consciousness, a living world reveals itself to you. Fears within you are dying. A new life is rising up in their place. You are passing through a crisis.

Rejoice.

Lovingly,
Mother Time

My dear One,

Each time you refuse to blame another and instead contain the pain and allow it to be transformed by the alchemy of Love, you discover the miracle of inner peace. A consciousness of Spirit emerges within your relationships that blesses and sustains them.

You are seeing that forgiveness is the process which allows this consciousness of Spirit—of soul time—to emerge.

Lovingly,
Mother Time

My dear One,

At this moment, as you pray for new life to be infused into a relationship, look out your window to the courtyard and see the drooping leaves of a palm tree branch being lifted up and spread out like wings by the wind. Now see them collapse and droop again as the wind dies down, then rise and expand once more in an alternating movement as the wind picks up again.

Be . . . like the wind . . . inhale . . . exhale.

When infused with Spirit, all things become new.

Lovingly,
Mother Time

My dear One,

"Love is an inner presence to all things," said a profound spiritual teacher. It has been revealed to you that, in truth, Love has no opposites. This means that all swings of emotion, all disease, all sickness, all sin, are false because they infer an opposite state.

In true Love, there can be no opposites at all. Keep this one thought constantly before you, and you will walk away from the false self that makes up a world of opposites.

Lovingly,
Mother Time

My dear One,

You are realizing that since Love has no opposites, every time you encounter a negative within yourself, you have slipped back into a self that you unconsciously made up of bits and pieces from past linear time. You have but to STOP and consciously let go of that old self, just as you would step out of an old, worn-out garment that no longer fits. Instead, step into a new and seamless gown. Love creates like Itself. If it has no opposites, then your true nature or soul has no opposites either—nothing negative to fix, heal, or mend.

Rejoice and be glad in this as you remember and re-member.

Lovingly,
Mother Time

My dear One,

The diabolic forces of your time that provoke fragmentation and disintegration seem to be dis-membering your family at this time. Like Osiris, the body of the family seems to be separating into fragments without any internal coherence.

You ask, "How can healing and resurrection be brought about?"

Like Isis, you must keep re-membering the whole.

In the meantime, tend to your grief of the moment.

Lovingly,
Mother Time

My dear One,

Your heart is heavy with sorrow at this moment. You are fearful for your loved ones. Go outward now and let the natural world heal you. Walk, and as you walk, listen—the birds are trying to sing to you.

The dove coos softly . . .

Ahead see a ruffled mushroom . . .

See a shaft of sunlight . . .

Smell the earth and carry a handful of it with you . . .

See three bricks covered with moss . . .

See an ant crawling trustingly on a leaf, its antennae out gently to find the next step . . .

Smell the fragrance of lilies . . .

See a snow goose floating serenely on the pond, her reflection perfectly mirrored in the water.

Hear the splash to your left . . .

See and hear a cardinal fluttering overhead . . .

See endless ripples in the pond before you . . .

Let yourself weep for all. For a culture dangerously out of balance. For a culture seeking sanctuary in the twenty-first century without knowing where to find it. For a culture that has forgotten the natural world is a major source of healing.

Help us discover it, you pray—the healing balm that will ease the terrible disorder of our time, the pain between one another, the destruction of the earth.

Dare to seek that balm for yourself. Dare to ask to find holiness in this moment. Ask where to look for it. Have the courage to give over your dark inner pictures. They come from a mind that has forgotten Love's capacity. Fear of the future has caused the conditioned mind of linear time to be activated. All you can truly say is that you do not know what the future brings. You can only place the future in the hands of the Divine . . .

Listen to the tree frogs' encouragement, the birds' cheerful song—they do not know the future either and still they sing.

See the maple trees bend down to the water.

See the fish leap up, causing bubbles to float lightly on the surface of the pond.

See two ants meet and greet each other on the tree beside you. They stand up, embrace lightly, then go busily on their way.

Feel the cool breeze.

Keep asking for the peace of Love to surround you. Here in this place, with life teeming around you, ask to *see,* ask to *feel* infinite blessings. Memorize the tree in front of you so that if you ever return to this place, *you will find that you know it by heart.*

A dragonfly zooms by. The breeze creates a dance of the maple leaf touching the water.

YES, say the bullfrogs.

YES, answer the birds.

YES, whispers the breeze.

YES, sing the crickets.

"YES" means trusting in the Divine process, in the Divine order that makes all things right. In this sacred moment, your seeing reunites the spiritual and natural worlds.

> Lovingly,
> Mother Time

My dear One,

Be willing to pray that the generational genocide that has brought about misery and destruction of human life ceases in your family. Open the dark hospital rooms of the past and allow the Light of Love to come in, and you will see gratefully rising those shadowy ancestors whose harmful patterns you have unconsciously perpetuated for so long.

Release them to their further soul evolution, and you will also be releasing the generations that follow.

> Lovingly,
> Mother Time

My dear One,

You have asked to see a new vision of "family" in soul time.

The old linear time notions of family based on assigned roles and the distribution of power that consciously or unconsciously manipulates and controls the family unit is disintegrating. In its place, a new understanding is emerging of family as a loving community of souls in one another's keeping. Everyone shares a deep faith and love in the truth of one another's connection to the Divine source.

This "new soul family" knows that at the soul level, there are no separate interests among them. Each family member shares a common engagement in moral struggles, always searching and sharing with each other the highest good. They relinquish false comparisons and inequities. They hold back neither hard truths nor loving support for each other's unique gifts. When forgetfulness comes, as it will, the "new soul family" holds each one in their hearts with love until remembering and vision return.

The "new soul family" remembers its interconnectedness, knowing that the whole is affected by every thought, word, and deed of each individual member so that each is required to assume personal responsibility without blaming others. The "new soul family" practices forgiveness as a way of life, fully realizing the struggles inherent within family dynamics and always seeking a deeper understanding of one another within the context of each relationship.

The "new soul family" does not fear vulnerability but rejoices in the openness and healing that it brings. The "new soul family" is conscious of its need to break harmful family patterns from the past, so each family member is free to grow on in their own soul evolution. They know that their common task is to allow an interior center to form from their mutual conscious interactions so they may continually evolve according to Love's plan inscribed in their hearts. They know that from this strong center, they all may face outward to the World Soul with an unshakable strength and wisdom informed by the power of Divine Love.

Lovingly,
Mother Time

My dear One,

One cannot realize the sacred depths of the other unless one realizes it in oneself.

True intimacy is the acknowledgment of the interior presence of the other.

Lovingly,
Mother Time

My dear One,

Can you begin to accept the soul struggles of your family without resistance?

Can you simply accept everything as it is right now?

Can you hold the conflict without trying to resolve it?

Can you hold to the truth that Love is working silently to heal all relationships?

Can you also speak the deepest truths you know when it is required of you?

You are being invited to take yet another step into radical trust.

Remember—Divine help supports your way.

Lovingly,
Mother Time

My dear One,

In response to your question about "a time to break down, and a time to build up"—these words:

Linear time produces a world built on acquiring, grasping, clinging.

∾ It separates us from Spirit, one another, and the world.

∾ Life is seen solely as an external physical event excluding feeling, sensing, imagining.

∾ Bodies jostle one another.

∾ Minds lock each other into cages.

∾ Separate egos and rampant individualism impose forms of domination.

∾ Imbalance, fragmentation, and breakdown of relationships.

∾ Hearts shrink, souls retreat.

∾ Latent seeds go unfertilized, unnourished, unwatered, unable to give birth to Love in and of the world.

∾ Accelerating linear time propels egos forward into cyberspace or backward into endless stale repetitions.

∾ Linear time deadens and dead ends.

All who suffer deep grief of heart and soul, pain of separation, misunderstanding, loneliness, bewilderment, anger, guilt, fear, STOP . . . Interrupt linear time. Step out of line and allow your wounded heart and soul to take you into the spiraling descent that grants access to the hidden depths of soul time.

There in the darkness find Light. There in the darkness find connection to Spirit and all living things. There, find Love's living presence underlying, overlying, encompassing, permeating, holding all things, rebirthing all things, guiding in all ways.

From the frantic crowded tempo of linear time rest awhile with me in the huge temple of soul time. Release endless decisions for the future and stale analyses of the past and be present with me in this holy moment, for it contains ALL fullness to meet every need. Beyond every thought of linear time, I wait to take you into a future unfolding with grace born of our eternal connection. You have only to let go and accept.

For your increasing efforts in seeking me within all relationships, I give thanks. Now, I will help you to transform your bitter cup into a chalice filled with healing balm.

∾ I will teach you to let me enter into hollow spaces in relationships.

∾ I will show you how to gently care for the delicate tissue of soul connections between you and the other.

∾ I will teach you to trust whatever comes out of these soul connections.

∾ I will teach you to hear disguised cries for help in anger and softly respond.

∾ I will teach you how to *see* with the other's eyes and *hear* with the other's heart.

∾ I will help you tiptoe behind words of the other and discover the Being there as the Being of yourself.

∾ I will help you accept all things exactly as they are, trusting always in my power to heal.

∾ I will teach you how to touch . . . and how to bless in the touching.

∾ I will teach you how to extend peace to the other.

∾ I will teach you how to surround the other in Light.

∾ I will teach you how to create a safe space in which the seeds of the soul of the other may be fertilized, watered, and nourished.

The soul's deepest longing is for the true recognition of one's spiritual nature. To achieve this re-cognition, souls must enter into the cauldron of relationship.

True re-cognition depends on releasing the past and the future and living in the present holy moment. To truly re-cognize is to heal and be healed.

As you return to play your part in the great unfolding cosmic drama between linear time and soul time, listen past the shifting thoughts of the ego to my still voice and let me lead you. Linear time will enlarge to the spaciousness of soul time each time you remember I am hidden in the present moment waiting to be brought forth. I will help you release the past and teach you to trust the unknown future by entering into the present moment where the newness of life resides.

Let the elements also come to your aid. Allow water to cleanse you, fire to purify, and air to lift you up to see from a distance. Allow the earth to reveal lessons of vulnerability, strength, gentleness, perseverance, endurance, constancy, trust.

Now, ascend on the eternal spiral into a world of soul time where healing, creating, and releasing connect you to Spirit, one another, and the world. Here, life is a spiritual activity, and the body a manifestation of soul. Here, seeing comes through the eyes of the senses, the imagination, the heart.

∽ Bodies gently touch one another.

∽ Minds let cages vanish.

∽ Individuality and mutuality expand as souls connect with Spirit in support of one another.

∽ Feelings, balance, and integration occur naturally.

∽ Hearts expand, souls advance, and relationships grow into new form from a common Inner Source.

∽ Seeds are fertilized, watered, nourished, and able to give birth to Love in the world.

Soul time opens new possibilities for renewed life.

Lovingly,
Mother Time

My dear One,

You see that linear "clock time," with its adherence to tasks before relationships, is threatening you again, and you are feeling great internal dissonance. At this moment, STOP and find the congruence between the deepest values of your soul and your actions.

Finding that congruence which is the exact match, the perfect correspondence between the outer and the inner, is the only task for which you need time. And soul time will provide it.

Lovingly,
Mother Time

My dear One,

"Ask and ye shall receive." Ask to see . . . surprises, particu-
larities, discoveries . . . and it shall be so. Vision is transformed by
the world, and the *world* is transformed by vision. The union and
re-union of the individual soul and the World Soul creates a deep
intimacy in which healing can come . . .

Lovingly,
Mother Time

My dear One,

I must say, you do resist doing what is best for you. You allow
your mind to hurl forth at such alarming speeds that the wisdom that could bring you health and peace cannot function. It
will only function as you STOP and quiet your mind and your
body.

You are being invited now to accept your own spiritual
wholeness, taking your place as it were, in the full scheme of things.
It means that you will no longer identify yourself entirely with your
body, your conditioned mind, or your fluctuating feelings. Instead, stand tall with all those who accompany you. The time
has come to separate yourself from past linear time and move
fully into the present moment of soul time with all its blessings.
It means you have been made ready through your willingness to
give over to Spirit, and are now ready for a new life of untold joy.

"Behold the old passeth away and all things are made new."
From now on, you will sense a continuous connection to those

in soul time who walk with you. At any time, you may call on them for guidance and wisdom, and they will answer.

You have asked to learn the real meaning of Love, and you are being answered. You see now that Love is constant and continuous—never changing, never wavering. It is a knowledge that you carry because you have experienced it so many times in so many countless ways. In the same way, you must Love with the same steady, unwavering constancy every single aspect, every single person in your life.

You are being given the privilege of knowing that everyone on Earth is equally loved and blessed. Though all have a spiritual identity, comparatively few remember it, believing themselves instead to be less. Even those who seem arrogant with power are acting out of a feeling of loss of their spiritual identity. There is a great grief in the world because of this sense of loss, and the time has come when the connection to the spiritual world must be recovered. Each soul must take up the task of this recovery.

Soul time, as I have told you before, is used in behalf of the recovery process. The purpose is to heal and create.

Lovingly,
Mother Time

My dear One,

You are wise to disengage yourself from the tentacles of the mood that has you in its grip at this moment. Like an octopus, it fastens on and holds you tight. You have the power to free yourself from it—not through vicious struggles, but by simply floating quietly on your back and letting it swim away.

Lovingly,
Mother Time

My dear One,

STOP—right now where you are, and drop all that you are groaning under. Let your load slip from your tired back with a thud and breathe deeply for a time at the side of the road. Now become aware of a tiny footpath on your right that you have seen before on previous descents into the valley. Let your body, now lightened, follow the footpath as it rises into higher altitudes where it leads you to a sunny meadow and children at play.

From a distance, look back on the rut-filled road you left behind and now . . . go join the children at play!

Lovingly,
Mother Time

My dear One,

Can you allow the natural world to heal you? Can you learn deeply that the trees steadfastly comfort you, the mountains stand sentinel over you, the streams cleanse you? Each leaf and rock remembers who you are as you pass by and rejoices as your soul moves ever more deeply into the soil of your own life.

You are being asked to let go completely of the self you made up so that the soul-spirit within you may be brought fully into existence.

You continue to try to live your life in the old ways, with all the worries, cares, fears, and worn-out perspectives that you have carried for so long as the physical manifestations that accompany them become increasingly painful. Can you not see that the old way has ended? You can not go backward, nor would you want to. Growth in soul time is measured by what you can let go of, in opposition to success in linear time, which is measured in terms of what you can acquire.

Every day in your prayers, ask what you can release, and you will be shown. The natural world will assist you here, for it yields and allows its transformations to take place in the endless cycles of birth, death, gestation, and rebirth.

Listen, learn, and yield for your life's sake.

Lovingly,
Mother Time

My dear One,

Alone at the end of this island with frigate birds above you, step out of your dark shroud of worry about finding "your place," your right context, and the feelings of alienation and separateness that accompany these thoughts. Right now, step into a new garment in which these words are sewn into the hem, "Love has no opposites." See how instantly negative thoughts and feelings vanish. In the mightiness of this truth all dualities disappear.

Both thoughts cannot coexist; the lesser fades in the Light of the greater, and you can see again from a distance, just as the frigate birds who are circling above you.

They know their place.

Lovingly,
Mother Time

My dear One,

You have discovered a truth about the healing of perception. When you returned in memory to the child within you and loved her through her struggles, supported her through her crises, strengthened her convictions, affirmed her essence, and comforted her grief over betrayals, you brought wholeness and forgiveness to your soul. The emotions engendered in childhood will no longer devastate you. Through Love, not sentimental love, but the deep Love of the Spirit within soul time, you will no longer identify with those negative emotions.

You see now that the child you *were* survived because of the *soul-spirit* you were *becoming*. Your child of the past intuitively knew that there was hope because she sensed a future that was coming toward her even when there were no signs pointing to it. Her unconscious childlike faith and trust in a process of growth kept her alive. Do you see, she trusted you, just as you are continuing to trust the presence of your future self as you see her more clearly now?

Lovingly,
Mother Time

My dear One,

The soil of the inner life must be turned over again in preparation for a new planting. Allow the process of transformation to unearth the deep layers that must be broken up and fertilized before the tender seeds of the future can grow.

Lovingly,
Mother Time

My dear One,

Today is a new day. You do not know what adventures it holds for you. You do not know what will come up for you to meet, either in the external or internal world. I remind you that you are truly a child on a journey into the greater life of soul time which exists within, but of which few are aware. To take along, you have been given this truth: You have within you, as does every soul, a power strong enough to meet any challenge.

Let your prayer for today be, "I am fortified with a shield of Light as I go forth. Let it illumine those things I need to see. Let me see them with Light. Let my loving gaze bless all that I look upon this day. Let no dark thought have room. Let me abide instead in the clear inner dwelling place of soul time where there exists no judgment but only Love and wisdom. Let me be empty today of all but that holy awareness."

Lovingly,
Mother Time

My dear One,

You have noticed that you bump into the past every time you strain toward the future. You will eventually learn that in the interior life, the future grows organically out of the *present*, which is what needs your attention.

"Realists" and "pragmatists" will scoff if you attempt to defend this. They will say that there must be goal-setting and future-planning if anything is to be accomplished. Soul time is quite a different way to live *one day at a time*, attuned to one's Spirit, and entrusting the unfolding of one's future to that same Holy Spirit. But I am telling you, this is the way of faith and the only *real* security.

The present *aware* moment is the only time in which change can be realized, and out of that change a new future, unlike the past, can emerge—a future that does not come out of old habits and patterns of linear time but a new understanding of the function of time itself which, as I have told you many times, is for creating and healing of the mind, body, soul, and world.

Lovingly,
Mother Time

My dear One,

You forgot that *your* happiness is *your* responsibility. You falsely "sacrificed" your time without speaking up and *acting* on your own convictions. No one else is to be blamed for your state of mind. The principle is movement, which involves both body and soul. Where there exists no movement, stagnation occurs. You needed to *move*. Today in the external world, there is much change and, consequently, much movement. The direction of that movement is not clear because the movement has not been accompanied by the understanding of the inner movement of soul time in its direction toward increasing clarity, increasing understanding, increasing Love. In order to learn these things, one must become aware of the presence of inner processes that work unceasingly to bring them about.

This day, choose consciously to be in conjunction with those processes or activities of the Spirit within soul time. At every moment, ask for the qualities you need to manifest, and they will be there for you. Straight from the temple of soul time, they will appear to assist you like a phalanx of soldiers sent to guard you safely on your way. Be not afraid. Each day is a new and glistening piece of marble that awaits your sculpting of it.

A bird just flew by the window in front of you, but you cannot follow it. Let go of your thoughts in the same way. Stay where you are bringing Light into every aspect of your life—the movement of the pen across the paper from left to right, the sounds of your loved one moving about, the steady beat of your heart, the twitching of your nose, the mystery of the day before you.

Remember—the Spirit is higher than the human soul. You can do something. You can always move upward to meet it.

Lovingly,
Mother Time

My dear One,

You see your mind, body, and soul as being heavy at this time, and we who support you on inner levels would lift your burdens from you if you would allow us to. We are waiting to receive them now so that you may go on with a loving, trusting heart into the greater Light of Spirit.

You are learning to understand by now how your thoughts influence your actions, but you have not understood as well how your actions influence your thoughts. You do not understand the degree to which you have outgrown parts of your old personality from linear time.

Once you completely release the past and allow the spiritual present to come into your life, your energy will return. You cannot experience synchronicity if you are living in past patterns. In fact, you cannot create at all in a true sense because linear time is holding you back. Your actions, you see, must be congruent with who you are now, not the you from the past.

Even the slightest repetition of old behavior can send you into a downward spiral. Your Spirit will contract, your thoughts will spin, and your body will register pain. Joy and healing are your functions on Earth.

Ask yourself again, "What brings me real joy? When do I experience healing and release?"

You have to learn again to move in the direction of your deepest interests, for that is where the life force of the Spirit in soul time is to be found. I must tell you that you have not done enough to claim your deepest needs, which is to say you have not yet done enough to embody your spirituality for yourself or for others.

You must ask for what you need at every twist and bend of the path.

"Seek and you will find."

Lovingly,
Mother Time

✍

My dear One,

You say you are determined to *see* things differently. Today let your desire be to see peace and harmony and notice what happens. Immediately in your room, you see the peacefulness of sunlight coming through the window on the chair where your loved one dozes. Now you notice the rose colors of the cushions hanging on the balcony outside and the way they harmonize with the deeper rose color of the chair. Next, you notice sunlight on the sculpture of a Native American woman and her child and how the child seems to be sleeping peacefully in her arms. Next you see the green leaves of the ficus tree in the corner and how they create a perception of depth with the trees outside the room and beyond.

What you desire to see you will see, not in fantasy, but in reality. The invisible world becomes visible. It is there all along, obscured only by meaningless thoughts that keep it from revealing itself. Do not be dis-couraged when you forget that *you* are responsible for the way you see your world, but simply STOP. Begin again with the truth that you have discovered, which is that the world you see reflects back to you the thoughts you make up.

If above all else you desire peace, you will find it. I repeat, "Seek and you will find." *The holy in the midst of life will reveal itself to a soul determined to see.*

What you see will be joined by all in soul time who are present with you in your determination.

Lovingly,
Mother Time

My dear One,

You ask where all this struggle is taking you. It is taking you to perfect peace, perfect surety, perfect trust in the exquisite process of life itself. Listening to the voice of Spirit within soul time and acting on it brings a state of mind, which is the final blessing of life. What begins as a tiny spark becomes a steady fire that consumes self-doubt, despair, and guilt in its flame. One becomes certain in faith as the knowledge and understanding of soul overtakes the tinier voices of the conditioned self. One reaches the field of silence where all voices are still, and all words come to rest. In that silence, one breathes in joy. One knows deep renewal and reunion of the soul with the Spirit in soul time.

In the stopping place of this holy moment, all is healed. The past is brought to the present, and in the encounter, a new future is born. One rests in this newness of life, assured that the darkness has been necessary to bring all to Light. Now one knows the everlasting connection with all that is. One's human nature becomes identical with nature itself. Rotations and rhythms of inner experience match cycles and rhythms of the earth. One feels the contractions and expansions, metamorphoses, and the same pulsating energy in one's body that exists in the throb of the earth.

The struggle is taking you to gentle laughter at the simplicity of it all. Vision comes in small glimpses and then gradually larger openings until it encompasses the whole.

The strivings of the soul are greatly honored, my child. Each small glimpse of hope that you receive must be shared so that the vision may come to all who seek as you do.

Be not discouraged if vision comes and goes.

> A ship moving in deep waters
> in darkness of the night
> receives only intermittent signals
> from the Lighthouse,
> but that is sufficient to bring it
> safely into harbor.

Lovingly,
Mother Time

My dear One,

The task is to see with double vision—to see with inner and outer eyes. Acknowledge first the ground of your own being, the soul instrument which registers the moment in all its fullness. Let your breathing match the breath of the natural world around you.

Next, become aware of the report of the senses. Hear the distant hum of a passing plane, the closer sounds of the tree crickets, the more subtle sound of a branch from one tree gently settling over the branch of another. Hear the wind and see the branches and leaves lift up in expectancy. See the tree before you with its divided trunk, one gnarled branch twisting upward, the other smooth branch moving in the same direction.

Become aware of the new untarnished holy moment made possible *by the meaning you give to it* and give thanks. "With an eye made quiet by the power of harmony and the deep power of joy, we see into the life of things," wrote the poet William Wordsworth. In this moment, you bless the earth, and it blesses you in return.

NOW moments exist at the meeting place between inner soul time and outer linear time. Turn and look behind you and see yet another whole world from another perspective. Hear the tall pines bend and sway in a delicate dance with each other. Beneath them, the hardwoods crisscross in random order. The sounds of the crickets are replaced by the melodies of birds in a rhododendron thicket. Behind you the kingfisher chatters in the stillness. Your soul breathes thankfully and quietly.

Only when one begins cultivation of one's inner Divine capacities does the universe change. That is the secret. At first, it reveals its grosser forms but then shyly offers up its details, its smells, its comforts, its intricacies, its wounds, its varying rhythms of movements and sounds, its Love.

Lovingly,
Mother Time

My dear One,

You cry into the night for solace, for comfort, for hope, for Light, when all about you seems to be flying apart, separating, disintegrating within every aspect of family, state, nation, and international life. You say you feel smothered by heavy blankets of darkness pressing against you now, but I tell you to peer out from under the covers. Look deeply into the night and become aware of the warm breath of early spring and the bright full moon surrounded by clouds that create a peach-blue aura around it. At this very moment, can you breathe into the stillness and know that all is embraced by Love?

Only from a still mind can the healing power of Love in soul time come to Light and overcome the darkness.

Be still and know.

Lovingly,
Mother Time

My dear One,

Your present struggle must be honored by being made very conscious. Once again, you meet the shadow side of yourself that has been aroused by your recent encounter with another. See the ominous figure of guilt that you have created from bits and pieces of your past—a mechanical robot patched together from the scrap heap of your mind. Hear its metallic voice demanding more and more of your time in slavish sacrifice to "good works," and hear its scathing indictments when you claim time for your own renewal, your own spiritual needs.

Dare to claim what you know is true for yourself despite the shrieks of guilt. Express yourself clearly. Tell guilt that despite all the pain and the problems of the world, you have chosen to follow joy.

You are at a crossroads on your journey now. We see you bending down to discover the way forward. Open your hand and receive the thread you have lost.

The world, as you see it now, is weary and without hope and without joy. No amount of good work done without joy can help it in the deepest sense. It must have the help that comes from hearts made joyful by the knowledge that Spirit dwells within each soul, from hearts that can see Love in all things, all people, all circumstances. For only in recovering its spiritual connection can the soul-sickness of your time be healed.

Your task is simple: be joyful and reflect that joy to others each day. This will do more good than you can yet imagine. Love will work its miracles through you, and at the crossroads, you will discover that against the high sweet song of joy, the shrieks of guilt will fade away.

Lovingly,
Mother Time

My dear One,

As in all matters, it is critical to know when to say yes and when to say no.

Right now, say "NO" to negative thoughts that would sneak in like thieves in the night and steal your peace of mind. In the past, you have entertained them like honored guests, handing over your valuables to them with no resistance whatsoever. You have funded strength enough now to stand up to them and to call for help in banishing them.

My dear, install an even stronger security system.

Lovingly,
Mother Time

✎

My dear One,

All things are lessons Love would have you learn, as is the recent inner tumult you experienced. Rejoice that you have the capacity to stay with your feelings, trusting the activity of Spirit to transform them. A poet once said, "Feelings are more demanding than thought. Thought is a flash of lightning. Feelings are a ray from the most distant of stars. They require all or nothing. They demand strength."

She might have also said that *going through* feelings to get to the other side of them *develops* the strength and courage to speak the words that come from your heart.

Feelings also take time, but, my dear, that is much of the healing work of soul time . . .

Lovingly,
Mother Time

✎

My dear One,

The problem for you, as it is for every soul that comes this way, is that you are not yet able to "see" enough. That is, you believe that the moment you are in will remain static as it is now, when in truth, it will change and transform itself just as a heavy thunderstorm becomes a clear sky. Your work is to keep knowing that every inner obstacle on your path will be removed without your involvement if you will simply get out of the way and allow Love to work in your life.

Go about your life as usual, paying particular attention to those matters and those others who call to you each day, while always trusting the process of change. Scientists talk about the changes taking place at the sub-atomic level of organic matter. Human beings, also of organic matter, are constantly undergoing a transformational process, though as yet few are conscious of it or understand it as a spiritual process as well. You are trying to do so, and I say to you right now, Wait and trust that process.

Lovingly,
Mother Time

My dear One,

When you forget and gallop off with the ego, you tend to slip off into the past of linear time where old habits of consciousness rise up. You see nothing as it is now, and act only out of past patterns of thought and behavior.

But *if* you learn to recognize what is occurring as you feel yourself charging off, you can return to the present moment with its unique fullness. When you are in soul time, you are able to see the past without bitterness, pain, or regret, and are able to face the future without fear.

It *does* require that you slow down so that you may learn to recognize your more subtle perceptions.

Lovingly,
Mother Time

My dear One,

You are now beginning to understand the enormity of your journey, which is everyone's journey, and why you must acknowledge the truth you have discovered and the gains you have made. The world, tired and hopeless, needs whatever truth each soul gleans from its individual journey through darkness to Light.

You *see* now that the function of time is to bring each soul to the awareness of soul time, which is the presence of holiness-wholeness. The way is to let go of all of your conditioned thoughts from linear time and trust that in each moment, you will know what to do, say, and think.

If you practice doing this, you will learn to forgive, and this, my dear, is the great secret. Forgiveness allows you entry into soul time, a world of extraordinary beauty where you see all people, things, and events bathed in a holy Light. To paraphrase an old hymn by Henry Walford Davies, "Love is in your eyes and in your seeing. Love is in your ears and in your hearing. Love is in your mouth and in your speaking."

From the center of soul time can come forth healing in forms that will continually be made known to you. You will help each soul that comes to you recognize itself and realize its own gifts, for each is a precious part of the Mind of Love, and each is truly holy. You will not need to strive. All will be effortless as you help each one discover the holiness of soul time.

Lovingly,
Mother Time

My dear One,

Do you notice how dis-Spirited you seem to be at this moment? Without a doubt, you have fallen into a slump. You have gone backward to "see" a time different from the one you are experiencing now and judged it as better than this one, thereby creating an error that is causing you pain. You are clinging to the past of linear time instead of attending to the presence of soul time.

Negative feelings of sadness and loneliness are welling up to sweep you under, but this time there is no need to "go under" with them. Recognizing them for the counterfeits they are, you can refuse them entry, knowing they will merely lead to self-pity, a pattern of thought that often plagues you. Each such thought pattern such as this is like a well-trodden path from linear time leading you downward—a path that your mind simply follows because it is familiar. Your creative task now is to discover new trails leading upward where the air is clean, pure, and better for breathing.

Turn your attention outward.

Take a walk.

Blaze a new inner trail.

Lovingly,
Mother Time

My dear One,

You are pondering a challenging moment of inner obstruction as you stand above the swirling pond. You struggle to plan ahead but meet with resistance at every turn. Fatigue and discouragement seem to accompany every effort you make.

Instead of struggling against them, try honoring them. Dare to rest instead of pushing ahead. Trust the activity of Love to show you the way as this moment dissolves into the next and the next and the next.

Remember how water circles and swirls around rocks of resistance.

Rather than solve—dis-solve.

Lovingly,
Mother Time

My dear One,

On your walk through this wooded area, you discover trees standing pale with gray fungus. One that lies toppled before you has a hollow core that is rotting from the inside out. You wonder whether its roots could not reach deeply enough to their source where they could find their own internal nourishment and renewal.

You also see signs of new growth emerging from the decomposition and decay. Everything before you suggests there is a "both-and" in all of life.

Earth is teaching you now as you struggle with the dilemmas of your times.

Lovingly,
Mother Time

My dear One,

The pilot announces that your plane is being rerouted because of heavy storms and turbulence ahead. Think of this as a help to you as you struggle at this moment with your own inner thunderstorms from the past.

Seek another altitude to fly above them into soul time, and you will find a new, less turbulent route.

Lovingly,
Mother Time

My dear One,

You speak of feeling overwhelmed by "too many demands pressing in on you," and I say STOP. Look outward, and see what you can receive in this very moment. Through your window, see the tall pine tree against the gray sky holding very still as the rain presses hard against it. Now watch as separate branches of the tree begin to dance, waving to each other as the wind presses in upon them. And now see a single bird soaring across the scene on its way to a purposeful somewhere despite the pressures of air currents against it.

Let go . . .
   Look up . . .
     Dance . . .
       Soar . . .

Lovingly,
Mother Time

My dear One,

Keep the faith—especially now when you feel yourself surrounded by darkness. Listen! Past your grief, past your pain. Listen to the darkness and hear the night crickets sing and the tree frogs croak. Let them into your heart; let them comfort you.

You encountered a situation which set you back in linear time—a situation in which you did not bring your wholeness to bear but allowed the ego to enter. It is often difficult to discern how crafty the ego can be, using even "good works" to perpetuate itself.

You are learning to see its tricks and step aside. You can no longer tolerate its behavior. You have come too far, and when you do not recognize the ego at work, your backsliding is more painful than ever. You see nothing but the past. You see nothing as it is now.

Now you have an opportunity to let go of past linear time thoughts, to let go of all situations which would allow the ego to ascend. Ask for the Divine help you need, and it will be yours.

Listen once again to the chorus of crickets, tree frogs, and whippoorwills who have just joined in. They love the darkness and sing of their love.

Sing with them.

Lovingly,

Mother Time

My dear One,

Old thought patterns of linear time creep stealthily back when you are not aware that you have left the basement door slightly ajar. They sneak in to take up residence in the cellar and set about concocting their potions of fears and worries.

Open the door at the top of the basement steps and turn on the light to expose their shenanigans and watch them flee quickly away. Then descend into the basement, sweep it out, and lock the door tightly.

Lovingly,
Mother Time

My dear One,

Can you allow confusion over a decision to enter into your galaxy of thoughts and trust the chaos that ensues? Can you simply allow the soul to absorb the tumult and transform it into the appropriate answer for you? Can you also trust that the soul will distill the essence of your question and hold the right answer, offering it up at the time you need it?

Can you leave the stew simmering on the stove and go about your tasks?

Lovingly,
Mother Time

My dear One,

You say that you cannot get beyond this present block of guilt and shame that you are experiencing. The circumstances surrounding your life at this time have brought the past into sharp focus once again. You must understand that you are seeing nothing as it is now. If you did, you would see that guilt is gone, reduced to dust in a cave, and you would also see that what you are suffering from is a loss of connection to soul time.

Move your attention outward and allow it to rest tenderly on a single dried leaf on a small tree that is bending and swaying upward and backward in the breeze. Now become aware of other leaves and other trees dancing in unison in the sunlight.

Now the breeze dies down, and the leaves all cease their choreography and become still. Become as still as they, my child. Trust with the leaves that the movement of the breeze will return, and with it, the movement of your inner block.

Lovingly,
Mother Time

❧

My dear One,

You are trying to take bits and pieces of incoherence connected to recent events and construct a coherent picture. You are trying to create rich, clear meaning out of a situation that is fraught with murky undertones and muddled agendas of souls with very different aims from your own.

Let go and recognize that it will not work. Truth is simple. The situation you are trying to make fit your picture is complex. Your task here is to overcome that complexity by stepping aside from the images you have created—images of the way you *want* things to be—and see things simply as they *are*.

Lovingly,
Mother Time

❧

My dear One,

Each soul has certain qualities to embody. Yours in this lifetime is to embody joy in a joyless world. You ask how this is to be accomplished in a world full of the pain of disease, poverty, and corruption, but I must tell you that is exactly why you must bring in the invisible life of soul time.

By permitting yourself to be pulled into the negativity of the world, you give power to the forces of darkness. By demonstrating joy, you demonstrate a different kind of power, the power of the Spirit to conquer all things.

It is daring to claim, but such is your task. By so doing, you will release others to claim theirs. No, you are not ignoring the distress of your time. In fact, you are meeting it with the courage of faith that overcomes all things.

Look for joy today in the simple moments. Remember the basic law of perception: You will find what you seek.

Today seek joy.

> Lovingly,
> Mother Time

My dear One,

This day you feel your imbalance in the absence of the soul-spirit connection. Your thoughts are scattered and weak, your movements sluggish. You say you feel the absence of soul time. You blame your condition on an overcast day.

A moment comes when you turn your attention outward to a tree branch outside your upstairs window, which lovingly leads your eye to the pine trees in the distance. Beyond them, in the overcast gray sky, March birds rise up and dip down, leaving the outlines of their graceful movements behind in your mind.

Through another upstairs window, you see the tops of redbud trees that you could not see from the lower story of your house. You step out of your past state of linear time into the ALL of time and see your thoughts reflected in this particular unrepeatable moment.

You are beginning to understand that the responsibility for the soul-spirit connection is yours. The activity of Love in soul time is always present, but you must be willing to STOP to allow it to show you the way.

Lovingly,
Mother Time

⮔

My dear One,

Today you took your depression into the park and let it dissolve against the joy of seeing:

⮞A tiny bird bathing in a rain puddle . . .

⮞A shaggy-haired dog good-naturedly allowing himself to be pulled along by a small boy . . .

⮞A trumpet swan allowing two young children to inspect her at close range . . .

⮞Buds on bushes longing to burst open . . .

⮞A group of young boys riding bikes down rocky mounds of dirt . . .

⮞A juggler performing to a delighted crowd . . .

⮞Brightly colored rowboats crisscrossing the lake . . .

⮞An elderly man sunning himself on a bench . . .

"Seek and you will find" that the world is trembling in its eagerness to heal now in the moments that you are truly present to the ALL-ness of soul time.

Lovingly,
Mother Time

⮔

My dear One,

It has taken you a very long time to realize that sometimes the only prescription for you is to play! Your heart has been overtaxed and heavy for so long now that it longs for Light and joy. Every day now, your one assignment is to love your life and be *joy-full* in it.

Starting today, look about you and allow images or special moments to penetrate your soul as you rejoice deeply in them. Then tonight, as your day closes, allow those images and moments to return and bless your life with their presence. In such a way, you teach yourself to Love.

It has often been true for you (as it is for many others) that you have done violence to yourself by taking on too many projects and overextending yourself. You need to be sure that your "in-tention" precedes your "ex-tension," and that your intention is based on what will bless you as you bless others. When you abandon your own soul's needs for renewal, you cannot be truly helpful to others.

Let the natural world nourish you. Smell the earth, listen to the sounds, allow your love to envelop everything you see, and your love will be returned many times over. You will see that your cup runneth over—with more than enough to share with others.

Lovingly,
Mother Time

❧

My dear One,

Even though you have been on this inner path for so long, you still have a great deal of trouble submitting to the dark feelings that often beset you. You resist them, even though you know in your mind that going through them will bring you back into balance.

Today the feelings engulfed you, and you allowed them to do so without resistance. By so doing, you discovered once again the miracle of healing and the joy of restored wholeness. Tears often restore balance to the soul. In your tears and vulnerability today, you were able to allow a loved one to speak to you of her feelings, and in your receiving of that message, she was healed along with you. The inner pain passed through, and you regained inner peace. Do you see that reversal can come at the lowest point?

Remember this, and learn to trust your dark feelings.

Lovingly,
Mother Time

❧

My dear One,

Each day your task is to turn the darkness to Light. Some days the task seems Herculean to you, as it does today.

You are dreading a confrontation with another individual with whom you have had several unpleasant encounters in the past, and whose views are sharply different from your own. You are shrinking from what you perceive to be the power of that individual. STOP. *See* the impoverished and powerless image of yourself you are holding at this moment. Ask yourself if that image supports the development of the whole human being? If it does not, you must let it go, no matter how familiar it is to you.

Resolve to transform the situation. Right now, ask that you see it differently. Call once again on your inner resources for help, and help will instantly be yours. In doing this, you will redis-cover the mighty power of Love at work.

This is what it means to work in partnership with Spirit. The situation you dread will reveal a hidden blessing. Watch and see.

Lovingly,
Mother Time

My dear One,

Today there were many lessons for you that emerged from your general lack of awareness. As I have said many times, you are either in linear time or in soul time. When you are in soul time, life seems to "flow," events connect, all is well. When you are in linear time, it is the opposite. You have no soul strength to meet the demands of your day. Today you felt an awkwardness, a stiffness in your relationships with others. Your body felt heavy, your heart was sad, awareness was gone. You did not seek renewal in the natural world where you know it can be found.

This is meant to be descriptive rather than pejorative, my dear, but I must point out the vigilance required to take care of your soul forces to keep them strong and alert. Every day, no matter the cir-cumstances, you must begin your day with silence in which you center yourself in soul time. Following this, you must look ahead lovingly to your day, "seeing" in your mind's eye, all whom you will meet. Surround each one in Light as if they were in a photograph framed by light, and follow with a prayer to surrender yourself anew to meet each person and circumstance in love. When you are thus prepared, your whole day will go well because you are working *with* the spiritual forces instead of neglecting them.

As you persevere as a spiritual athlete, you will notice at more subtle levels the consequences when you neglect to practice. Today your practice was with heavy weights, which caused the stiffness you feel in your body and the awkward reactions you received from others. Tomorrow, imagine practicing yoga instead.

It *is* hard work, we know, but the work is inward as well as outward. Look both ways.

Lovingly,
Mother Time

My dear One,

You are learning to challenge every negative thought that emerges within you, realizing that all come from forces of past linear time, which would keep your soul from realizing its presentness now. These forces seem to be real because they carry with them an irrational feeling which seems to justify them. But if you stop and face them, demanding an accounting of their intent, they will disappear in the mists of illusion. They will dissolve away, and inner peace will return.

I must remind you over and over again of your own power to reverse the direction of your negative thoughts. STOP! Consider whether even your "justifiable" anger has value. Does it come from your interpretation or from fact? What are the consequences of it? And so on. Much thoughtlessness happens between two people who live as partners, but as consciousness increases, conflict diminishes, as indeed it should, but there will always be lapses.

Individuals are either in or out of awareness. The spiritual work, of course, is to stay conscious. If you find that your partner has lost awareness, do not follow them into the darkness, but hold onto the Light and they will often follow, for that is the spiritual law.

You can hasten that time by consciously holding the other in Light. By visualizing your loved one surrounded by Light, you will be practicing the skill of forgiveness.

> Lovingly,
> Mother Time

My dear One,

You know by now that you must completely let go of all that causes you anxiety and tension. You are called upon to accept joy and peace in their place, yet right now, it seems as if you are being required to abandon all you have worked for these many years, and so the ego is resisting fiercely. It has grown accustomed to identifying itself with your work in the external world, and it can not conceive of another life. Yet, let go it must if you are to live. It is a death that you are experiencing in order that a greater life may emerge, but you may only trust the truth of this statement at a later time.

You have suffered much pain and fear. You are ready in your conscious mind to let go, but your ego still has not received that message. Speak to it gently now and carefully explain what you have decided, as you would to a child. Very gently and very tenderly, you must say, "I have decided to live, to be healthy, whole, and happy now. I need for you to relax your grip and breathe deeply with me."

Once again, my dear, notice the natural world and its acceptance of life as a series of surrenders. Remember—you are part of that world.

Lovingly,
Mother Time

My dear One,

Stay very steady and quiet now as you navigate through the birth canal, so to speak. There is much travail at this time, and I will repeat once again: You must trust the process that carries you on. At the same time, you must remember deep compassion for others and their life processes—the struggles, the false directions, the illusions each soul encounters on its journey toward the Light of soul time. Reach out and give support and encouragement wherever and whenever possible, knowing that as you do so, you are in league with Divine forces.

You are living in a time that has forgotten the sacred. In the midst of this time, *you* must remember so that the spark of Spirit which is yours will not die, and so that your remembering will help others do the same. It is your redemptive task—*re-deem* means to see again. As you learn to see again and to share your seeing, you will be a blessing to those who came before you as well as those who will follow in the future.

Remember the sacred NOW as you see the land glimmering softly in the autumn light. See the cattle standing mutely, their breath rising in frosty wisps on a cold November day. See the colors of the fall leaves as they float softly to the ground. Hear your own heart beating in the same rhythmic cadence as the heartbeat of the earth. Allow the living, flowing fountain of life within you to aerate your soul, cleansing and purifying it of any toxins that may enter. Allow yourself to be healed and transformed, for that is the purpose of soul time.

Lovingly,

Mother Time

My dear One,

Concentrate now as never before on that which abides and not on what is passing away. Everything is always, at every moment, in a state of change and transformation. That which is lower ascends, that which is higher descends. The movement is continuous.

Now at your low point, you will begin to feel the upward movement of your energy. Trust this process completely. If you halt this natural process with judgments and interpretations, you will impede your healing. Turn your attention to finding your way back into harmony with the natural world, which is the same as being in harmony with your own biological rhythms.

Your compulsive patterns of behavior and your hectic pace in linear time have put you out of harmony with your soul. This has made you ill. The only way to restore your balance is through a complete letting go of all compulsive patterns, of all notions of control or manipulation of events, of all judgments, all attacks on yourself, and all planning for the future. Only in this way can the process of self-destruction be reversed.

Do not be dis-couraged. It is difficult for your ego to accept that it must go through these experiences after all it thinks it knows and has learned. These are battles that have been waged by all souls throughout time. You are on your way to moving beyond linear time to full recovery of heart, mind, and body. The body will become a comfortable home—a healing residence for spiritual activity—and you will become what you in truth already are—a blessing in your own life and in the lives of others.

Lovingly,
Mother Time

∞

My dear One,

Your state of mind is that of a caged animal pacing restlessly back and forth, back and forth. Your resentment at your present circumstances has created it so. You have not yet found a way to allow yourself space and time for your own deep needs, and this you must do. You have fallen into a false notion of sacrifice, and in your interpretation of that idea, it is unhealthy for you and those you care for. Can you begin to understand that if you continue in this way, you will set up dependent relationships? Is that what you want? Understanding this is essential for your spiritual well-being as well as for theirs.

People have very different needs. Learn to care for others lightly and lovingly, and while you do so, see all surrounded by Light. Walk out of the cage you put yourself in out of a sense of guilt and obligation. You do not belong in a cage but in open spaces where the wind blows and the sun shines. Listen as your feet kick up the dry leaves. See the long shadows of the pines before you and the dried maple leaves trembling in the January afternoon light. You are out of your cage now, walking in the woods where you are more natural and at home.

By releasing yourself, you release your loved ones into the care of Spirit, which allows their cages to vanish as well. Dwell together in the great open spaces of soul time where true freedom reigns.

Lovingly,
Mother Time

My dear One,

As I have tried to help you understand again and again, time is for the healing of all misperceptions of the mind. You have understood me only partially. There is so much for you to learn, for in believing that the mind is in the head, you have allowed the mind of your *body* to be neglected. The mind of your head is the same as the mind of your body—they are one and not two. You must now learn to connect your head and your feet, so to speak.

This is the incarnational task of this period in your life. You have reached a turning point. You cannot continue along in the same way you were going. Rejoice that you have reached this plateau and embrace it. See it as a great blessing and know that you have been given all the resources you need to continue toward new understanding.

When you hear my voice and know that it comes from your center in soul time and not from your head, you will shift the locus of all you think, say, and do.

> Lovingly,
> Mother Time

❧

My dear One,

Today a negative thought seizes your mind and threatens to hold it captive. Remember that thoughts have power only if you give them power. The ego feels threatened by your recent progress and is challenging you now. Rather than seeing this as an attack on your peace of mind, see the ego as you would see a little child who grabs a toy and then runs and hides with it. Sooner or later, if you pay no attention, the child will drop his toy and come back to see what everyone else is doing. Go on and do what you need to do today, and you will find the willful little child returning for your love.

Even now, the child watches for a signal that it is safe to let go of his game.

> Lovingly,
> Mother Time

❧

My dear One,

Those of soul time are returning home to a place which, in truth, they never left. They are discovering that time is for the healing of all wounds, all pains of the past, all misperceptions.

As each soul takes up her or his own healing task, the reverberations go backward and forward in time. Those who have gone before are blessed and able to move onward in their own soul evolution, and those who will follow are similarly blessed.

It is impossible for you to understand how mighty a task you are undertaking and how many are the companions who walk with you along the way.

Lovingly,
Mother Time

My dear One,

It is difficult for you to see how extensive is the depth and breadth of your own healing need. You have been so busily engaged in the external tasks of your life that you have not been able to see the inner tasks until now. You are now fully taking on the heroic task of yourself, trusting that somehow out of your own revelations, you may help others. If you only knew how significant that desire is, you would take new heart.

I can tell you that soul time supports you in your longing to break out of old patterns of thoughts and behaviors. You are right in identifying new directions in which you want to go and setting your intentions to start with them. It is important that you think of only one day at a time and that you move slowly and stop often if the intelligence of your body requires it.

You are now learning to integrate that soul intelligence.

Lovingly,
Mother Time

My dear One,

Yesterday you learned that accepting the depression that you felt within transformed it. You allowed the disowned part of yourself to simply be, and in so doing, the depression was lifted.

When you judge a part of yourself as negative and fight to transform it, it only becomes more overwhelming. Remember, "resist not evil." You have thought of yourself as a teacher, and now you are learning that in order to be a true teacher, you must become a true student.

Become vulnerable to each lesson that is given you daily, realizing that each day is a miniature of the whole of your life. You will be given exactly what you need to learn. Decide *with Spirit* what your intentions will be, and then review them at the end of the day with me.

Remember that you are supported by spiritual forces. In soul time, we rejoice at each clatter and clank that signals the break up of old habits, patterns of thought, and outgrown attitudes.

Lovingly,
Mother Time

My dear One,

You have done a good job of participating in your own healing process today with your most recent task, which was detaching yourself from the inner martyr that can have such a grip on you. You have come far enough on your journey of consciousness to recognize your negative patterns of the past. Whenever you no longer feel at peace, your thoughts become repetitive, your emotions churn, and your body tightens.

This time you wisely stopped and simply allowed the thoughts to come, noticed their content in a mildly curious way, and listened to their messages so that you could discern the subterranean old, dark crone that had you temporarily in her grasp. In this case, the messages were full of anger at another because you had "done so much" and had been "so disappointed by the lack of appreciation and enthusiasm for your efforts."

This is a common pattern of human nature, but in your case, it is quite over-developed. This time you were able to refrain from venting your indignation on others but retreated into your interior vessel and asked Spirit to let you see the situation differently. You then went about your work for the day, trusting that the transformation would take place.

An image came to you from the soul—the image of a huge granite block breaking up and disintegrating—and you began to feel your freedom returning. You now see more clearly that the inner work has to do with recognizing the dark figures from the past that comprise the collective consciousness of humankind, detaching yourself from them, and then trusting the ceaseless activity of Spirit to transform them.

In the future, my dear, do for others only with joy and without any conditions attached, and the martyr may be permanently vanquished.

Lovingly,
Mother Time

My dear One,

Your own negativity passes before you like a thunderhead on the horizon. Let it pass through your soul without letting it affect you. The storm would darken your world if you allowed it. There is too much to see here to permit your vision to be obscured. The forces of nature are always at work—within and without—wearing down the rocks on the beach, the sandstone on the mountain, and the negative nature of the conditioned mind.

Do not fear any part of the natural world. Much of humankind has excised it from the context of their lives. You must learn to include it. All of it. You are now connecting to the voice of the earth as it speaks through you.

Listen.

Lovingly,
Mother Time

My dear One,

We know that you are exhausted from encountering trials and tests, but you have been faithful in your quest to discover the meaning of time, and the trials and tests are part of that quest. Once, long ago, you asked for wisdom, depth, and magnitude, and they are being offered to you. Do not shrink from them now. You will overcome these tests because you have come far enough in your journey to understand your current situation.

Now you are being drawn by the attraction of guilt. Gaze upon it with the full power of Love and state clearly, "You have no power over me." Notice how impersonal guilt is in its attraction, how wooden and mechanical. It cares nothing for you, your loved ones, your work, or your life. Sever its head from its body, and you will discover that it is full of sawdust and shavings. There is no life force within it at all. See it crumble before you as it disintegrates and blows away.

As you perform this mighty act, know it is not for you alone but for others as well. Nothing is ever isolated in its effects. You will be serving humankind as you deal decisively with your own monsters. Above all else, you must want to be whole. That is what this time is for. The pain and suffering will end only as each individual takes on the mighty task of inner transformation. *Nothing else will do.*

Lovingly,
Mother Time

My dear One,

You are correct when you discern that your mind tends to wander aimlessly down paths that would take you away from a single focus on your deepest desire, which is that of inner peace. Keep repeating to yourself, "Above all else, I want the peace of soul time," and all thoughts that do not fit within this statement will drop off wearily like poorly disciplined foot soldiers who cannot keep up and desert into the hills.

Remember: Believe—be-*live*—and all will be well. When the time comes for you to know what to do and what to say, you will *know.* "Seek ye first the kingdom." Concentrate now on your greatest desire. Move into soul time where all thoughts may be brought to rest.

Lovingly,
Mother Time

∞

My dear One,

There is a wisdom in the body that you must learn to honor. For so long, you have ignored or abused the body by neglecting its needs, not heeding what you have put into it, constricting its movements, and unconsciously attacking it with your judgments and criticisms.

On many occasions, it has protested through its natural defense system, and you have responded temporarily to each of these by stopping and giving it attention. But then you have always returned to your old ways.

This will no longer do. Now you are required to learn to love the body so long despised. Each day you must bless it for its work on your behalf to promote health and healing. Take care of it, allow it to dance, to sing, to play. It also likes to listen in on our conversations!

The body of Earth is likewise protesting the ravages upon it. Can you learn new ways of caring for it too?

Lovingly,
Mother Time

∞

My dear One,

Today, we will attempt to speak of the unspeakable, that mysterious connecting principle of Spirit, which is ever active, ever changing, ever continuous in one's life. It is the primary interior secret that works to restore harmony, promote healing, and foster an awareness of kinship between the personal and the universal.

The connecting principle of the soul-spirit is that which links each soul to all who seek a common Story. One might think of it as an invisible thread that links together all threads. As the spider contains the potential for weaving a web as a manifestation of "spiderness," so does each soul contain the connecting principle of Spirit, which allows the creation of a unique expression of life. The creative principle makes itself visible and evident by attracting to your life all those people, events, and experiences that will aid in your inner growth.

How does this apply directly to you, you ask? It means that in every relationship, primary or secondary, your soul-spirit has the opportunity of making this connecting principle visible as you learn to trust the life process that makes it possible.

It's also called Love.

> Lovingly,
> Mother Time

My dear One,

You are wise to notice what constricts your awareness and what expands it. In that way, you will free yourself of unwanted patterns of reaction as quickly as they occur. Today, an old pattern came up from the basement of your mind. You registered it and then examined it later to discover the image behind your reaction. It was your old nemesis self-pity trying to pull you down. But this time, instead of allowing that to happen, you practiced seeing the thought as a gray, shrinking, contracting shape, then imagined seeing it billow out into shades of rose and pink. When the thought still tried to possess you, you handed it off to a passing hawk who flew off and dropped it into a mountain crevice.

You know by now that a thought can take hold, and for the time in which it possesses you, you are the "exteriorization" of that thought. But if you immediately begin to transform it, you will return to an expanded awareness, which is your greatest desire.

And never forget the Divine help that is aiding you.

Lovingly,
Mother Time

My dear One,

You are quite correct in estimating your present physical difficulties as a choice you have unconsciously made, and as such, you have the choice to decide differently. You must summon your imagination to your aid and allow it to illumine your experience so that you can see your present moment clearly. It will show you that you have given power to the idea of dis-ease and that you must now withdraw that power and place it in the stronger concept of health and well-being. The imagination, as revealer, will show you pictures of yourself functioning in effortless and healthy ways.

You do not realize the extent to which the unconscious controls until you detect it and bring the imagination of Love into greater ascendancy. This is the powerful truth that soul-spirit demonstrates—that each one has the potential within that can be called forth.

Remember that you are here to be healed completely—in mind, body, and soul.

Lovingly,
Mother Time

My dear One,

Your fears and the powerless image of yourself that you carry are illusions. Notice how faceless are the fears, how impersonal and mechanical, and then notice how diminished is the picture of yourself.

Learn to use the power of your imagination to see "differently," and the fears will vanish. "See" a monstrous fear coming at you and then imagine yourself running out to meet it with the gaiety and innocence of a child who claps her hands and watches in delight as the fear evaporates. Or, see it coming toward you like a huge wave that breaks at a distance on the shore and becomes only foam when it touches your feet.

Strengthen your soul forces through the power of your imagination. This is the work of transformation in soul time, my dear. The Light can always overcome the darkness.

Lovingly,
Mother Time

My dear One,

You are discovering that the imagination is not merely a mental faculty for producing fantasy and distortion or a gift of the talented few. In soul time, imagination is a Divine instrument for seeing and penetrating deeply into the reality of the world about you and is a direct link to your own unique interpretation of the world and your own soul essence. In other words, the imagination can connect you to all that is.

When imagination is unused or underdeveloped, it either atrophies or becomes negative, producing distortions called anxiety and fear. When honored and moved into its rightful position in the life of a soul, it offers the potential for transformation.

The individual soul, under the guidance of the imaginative faculty, can learn to see from a higher vantage point that brings healing and blessing. Imagination can take the individual soul beyond the misshapen personality form to see "the more" of all life in soul time.

Imagination acts as a reflector and interpreter that reveals a kaleidoscope of constantly changing images, opening doorways into the vast unknown. It is a verb, constantly active, and a noun, being acted upon. It is masculine—reaching out, extending, penetrating. It is feminine—passive, womblike, fertile, spacious. Imagination is the union of the two, capable of creating infinite responses and infinite forms.

When imagination is denied or suppressed, it can erupt into violence. When it is integrated into the whole life of the individual, it reunites soul with Spirit.

Imagination is a power—a reality that affirms the immanence of Love. It links the individual soul to the World Soul. It enables you to re-cognize—re-know—as you once did, that your true identity is Spirit.

Lovingly,
Mother Time

❧

My dear One,

There are few who would disagree that the "kingdom" is not yet come, yet I tell you that the kingdom of soul time *is* come if you could but see it. Or see into it. If you could but see the activity of every single thing about you, the molecular dance of the table in front of you, the life force of the plants on top of it, the soul capacity of a loved one in the next room.

Transformation exists in every present moment if you can but remember to look for it. If you allow your insights to extend to every living thing, you will come to know that all is alive as you acknowledge and affirm it. As you increasingly learn to "see" with new eyes, you will discover a reciprocity, a relationship, a friendship with all about you. You will then begin to fully understand that the "kingdom" is the *meaning* you give to all that is.

If you judge and condemn from conditional linear time thinking, that becomes your reality. If you allow the world to present itself to you, the "kingdom" of soul time will rise before you.

Lovingly,
Mother Time

My dear One,

Notice the heaviness of your dreary thoughts as they plod across your mind. Blame, Fatigue, and Anxiety are all staggering along a rocky road, full of bleakness and despair. Hear their pitiful messages and see the burdens they carry. Then watch with delight as a troop of young, light, loving, angelic spirits slip onto the scene, tiptoe up behind the melancholy company, and gently take their heavy burdens away as if they weigh nothing at all!

Instead, they give to each one a tiny star, light as a feather, and small enough to hold in their hands. Suddenly, Blame wears a seamless garment, Fatigue begins to walk with a lighter step, and Anxiety begins to dance. Before your eyes, the scene becomes transformed, and you rejoice.

You must understand by now that you have the power within you to see all situations differently. You can see with the judgment of linear time or with the vision of soul time. The choice is yours. You have been given the Divine gift of imagination. Use it wisely and well.

Lovingly,
Mother Time

❧

My dear One,

Try very hard to absorb these thoughts: You have unconsciously sought to make yourself and the world unholy by your unwillingness to learn that it is not so. All around you and within you, negative images arise. In the outer world, seeds of disaster, disease, and violence abound. *Within* you, anxiety, depression, doubt, and fear swirl. You mistakenly accept all of these as real, and by so doing, fail to activate within yourself the Divine reality of the spiritual life of soul time. The truth is that you and all of your world are holy. Everything that you can see or think of is holy. To understand this is to completely reverse your present way of being in the world.

You are here to develop a will that is in accord with the will of Divine Love by accepting with complete faith your own holiness and the holiness of all of Love's creations. As you do so, you will leave behind the negative world that you have made up out of scraps and bits and pieces from past linear time thought.

Let it go! Beginning with this moment, see a new world of soul time, clean and untarnished.

Put on a clean pinafore and accept yourself as a daughter of Love. See everything from this perspective. Look around you and repeat, "Everything I see before me is holy. The light coming through the window and the leaves on the trees. The ornate rug beneath my feet and the bright colors on the pillow as it catches the sunlight. A loved one is present in the room with me. Others are here with me in thought." Bless them as they come and go. Your mind is part of Love's mind and you are holy. You have but to remember this, and you will be richly blessed.

Let go of all "bad" and "good" labels that have crept into your consciousness. Accept your true spiritual heritage . . .

Lovingly,
Mother Time

My dear One,

About forgiveness, I can not say enough, for in truth, it holds a key to all that is important in your inner development. Through forgiveness, you will be able to "see" as you are intended to "see"—with the vision of soul time instead of the judgment of linear time. Instead of judging one another, which gives only a distorted perspective, you learn to see each other as you truly are—members of one family, each with particular talents and qualities, each with a highly individualized "lesson plan" to learn during a lifetime.

At any given moment, if you judge another, you are distorting a picture of the whole by substituting only a part for it. The other suffers, and so do you, taking on errors that will simply have to be corrected later on.

You can and must step aside from certain negative behaviors; you can and must speak clearly and forcefully to those behaviors while continuing to release judgment on the person. It is a discernment you are capable of learning, and it will save you much time and pain.

Lovingly,
Mother Time

My dear One,

It is important for me to talk to you about the assimilation of your experiences into memory pictures, which you can look on with joy and gratitude. Every experience must ultimately be "digested" and transformed into a spiritual reality. Does that seem too difficult? Surely, you say, some of the most difficult and bitter experiences cannot be seen from a spiritual perspective. I can only stay firm and ask you to look carefully at each of your difficult and bitter experiences as you feel strong enough to do so.

Seek outside help with this if you do not feel strong enough. These untransformed experiences carry strong emotions which must be released, and for this, you may need a loving physical presence—one who can create a non-judgmental space in which painful feelings can be safely released.

You must be willing to enter the void to be healed and cleansed. By going backward in time, so to speak, you not only change the past and present, you change the future as well. You will *re-vise*—re-vision—the way you "see."

You will learn to see that the situation that calls for forgiveness happened because the spiritual dimension was *not* brought into it at the time it occurred. Returning to it now *with* Spirit will bring you the healing you long for.

Soul time rejoices and supports your courage, and a new path opens before you while supporting the evolution of the cosmos. In doing the healing work of your time, and transforming the obstacles to loving, you participate in a greater work—that of letting the world be loved through you.

For such was humankind created, and you are continuing that creation.

Lovingly,
Mother time

My dear One,

Today you realized that you were still carrying unforgiveness toward one you thought you had forgiven completely. You were dismayed to discover a small dark closet where unforgiveness still remained hidden, and you were forced to open the door and allow it, shamefacedly, to come out and meet the Light.

Few realize how forgiveness must be practiced if the dark closets are to be cleaned out. Let me remind you of the mechanics of this practice. Allow the one you need to forgive to come into your mind and "see" yourself offering your hand to him or her. "See" with your mind's eye, the two of you standing together surrounded by Light, and simply hold that picture in your mind for as long as possible. When you have done that, you will come back to the present time to discover that your mind is free and your inner balance has returned.

How often must you do this, you ask? Until it becomes a way of life, and all the closets have been completely cleaned out.

Just remember that housekeeping is a daily task.

Lovingly,
Mother Time

❧

My dear One,

You are becoming increasingly aware of the relationship between fear and guilt. They are cohorts. They pal around together, constantly reinforcing one another. They are a lethal twosome against which each soul must be ever vigilant.

Don't wait until they strike, for then it is often too late to escape their vengeful moves. Be far ahead of them, asking for Divine protection against their onset. Self-knowledge is a powerful weapon here. Knowing what your particular fears are allows you to request reinforcements in the battles against them.

Never forget your own warrior nature.

Lovingly,
Mother Time

My dear One,

In this moment, it is a temptation to submerge yourself in a sea of feelings and allow "justifiable" resentment to pull you under. Instead, come up for air from the watery depths. Swim upwards until you break through into the bright sunshine.

You are being asked here to slip out of the clutches of the sea monster "martyrdom." Let your prayer be for inner detachment from all that would pull you backward into past patterns. Seek outer activities that will move you forward and renew your soul.

Lovingly,
Mother Time

My dear One,

You long to know how to "help" a loved one whose path of self-destruction has taken her to a crisis point. You know that neither emotional appeals nor coercion will do. You realize that the task before you is beyond any intellectualizing or "strategy," and perhaps is best given over to those with experience and skills that exceed your own.

Your preparation as you go to her now is of utmost importance. "See" your loved one completely without judgment of any kind. Know that before you stands a mystery of creation whose destiny is unknown to you. Remember that you have a soul connection to this individual. Trust in the living bond that ties you together, and pray to be fully present in the moments you share through this Divine connection.

Heaven supports your way.

Lovingly,
Mother Time

∾

My dear One,
The way you see depends upon who you think you are.
Love created you like itself.
The *way* you see affects *what* you see.
In all things, remember to see with Love.

Lovingly,
Mother Time

∾

My dear One,
You are aware of the forces of dis-integration within you and all around you—disturbing dreams, chafing tasks, negative reactions, battering personalities, the startling events of the time in

which you live—and yet I tell you that you must continue to gather yourself at the center of Love within soul time as you move into the outer world. By extending the center outwards, you spiritualize your world and transform your part in it.

The center of Love in soul time has a unifying power that can bring all fragments into harmony within it. It is the Universal expressing itself through you. Your one task is to continue to allow this activity to manifest in you by clearing away all obstacles to it.

Know that Divine forces go before you, strengthening and supporting you.

Lovingly,
Mother Time

My dear One,

By going deeply into the darkness, you are discovering the Light of soul time. In the midst of the sordid company of negative thoughts, you are finding the center of energy that unifies all things—the Divine principle of Love. You are reaching out to it and are being answered by it. In doing so, you are discovering the living presence of a past that now supports your journey, for you are willing to release it from its pain and bring it fully into the NOW moment. You have entered it and redeemed it by your willingness to see it in a new Light.

Memory of the past, you see, is not static and unchanging. It is alive and trembling in its desire to be transformed through a new understanding of it *in* the present *for* the present and *for* the future.

The human psyche contains within it all that it needs for its transformation. It simply requires your willingness in accord with Divine willingness to bring it about.

Lovingly,
Mother Time

My dear One,

Today you are discovering once again the miracle of the activity of Love within. You allowed the negative contents of your mind to run their course while you quietly went about your daily tasks. Although keenly aware of your negativity and disturbed feelings, you did not attack yourself or another, but simply observed them with a simple prayer to be allowed to see "differently" the situation that triggered it. You contained the negativity with faith that Love would transform it. And so it did.

The conditioned mind of linear time runs through the inner universe like a multicolored ribbon—now gold, now green, now black, now purple, now twisted in knots, now negative, now positive. When you release that mind to soul time, as you did this day, Love settles down softly, like a dove in the center of the heart, and all else disappears.

Lovingly,
Mother Time

My dear One,

In this moment, you are experiencing clarity of purpose and the quiet of your heart. You have come to a new understanding of sacrifice. Rather than dreary resignation and submission followed by feelings of anger and blame, you are seeing sacrifice in its true meaning, "to make holy," which is accompanied by feelings of joy. You are no longer splitting off a part of your inner life and denying it. You are instead claiming it and allowing it to live within you. You are giving it space to breathe and grow.

On a daily basis, you are seeing what it needs to be nourished and developed. You are tending it as you would a garden, actively seeking those people, experiences, and ideas which will help it grow. Continue to take loving responsibility for sacrifice as you would for a new infant.

Outside, a new moon rises over a dark lake.

Lovingly,
Mother Time

❧

My dear One,

Each time you allow yourself these communions, you are coming home to your Self—to the deep organic mind that continues within all of life and burns deeply within each soul on Earth. This is the true nature of every individual, although very few on Earth are as yet aware of it. Awareness requires a complete reversal of old patterns of thinking and being, a suspension of all judgments, and a willingness to live in total vulnerability with a deep trust of the unknown.

For those who embark on this journey homeward, all of heaven rejoices and sends Divine protection to lead the way. The cramped quarters of the ego, built on the sands of linear time, slowly give way, and out of the rubble of its disintegration, the temple built on solid stone becomes ever more discernible. As you allow time for me to enter your consciousness, that new form becomes stronger, for it is within these communions that you become aware of new relationships, the building blocks of the temple.

Lovingly,
Mother Time

My dear One,

You must continue to allow the space for me to communicate with you in order to keep your soul nourished. It is easy to fall back into old reflexes that keep you bound in the endless activities that pull you down into a vortex that drags you away from the soul time that can nourish and sustain you. Even "good works" will do this if they take on a momentum that drains your energies and weakens your heart.

When one is in linear time, the world is overloaded with horizontal activities that keep expanding at an exponential rate. What is desperately needed to create balance in your time is a verticality—knowledge and truth that can disrupt the mechanical and habitual activities of linear time and create a deepening of the soul.

Ask yourself what you can do to create inlets to the soul forces that can renew and restore you to the tasks of your time. From far beyond the repetitive escalation of horizontal time, soul time emerges—a time in which healing and creativity may flourish.

Lovingly,

Mother Time

My dear One,

Life is meant to be lived within the flow of soul time, and when your actions deeply satisfy your mind and heart, there is no need for thought. Only when you fail to achieve a response that feels right in a situation, do you need to stop and allow the organic processes of your inner life to assist you in your further development.

Today, out of a fear for the future that emerged, you reacted to a situation with emotions that had their genesis in the past. You "fell" into linear time, and your soul temporarily lost balance. You wisely stopped and turned your attention inward, releasing its narrow focus, and enlarging it to encompass the colors, textures, and movements of the NOW moment.

Do you see how your balance is regained as you increasingly learn to move into soul time?

Lovingly,

Mother Time

My dear One,

Your inner kingdom is strengthened each time you are able to overcome an old linear time pattern of thought with a newly discovered inner image of renewal. To help you, I will offer this picture: Imagine Love as a giant searchlight firmly anchored at the center of your soul time. See how the light sweeps into every crevice of your inner landscape and then does the same over your outer landscape, illumining all that it touches. If there is even a scrap of guilt or pain on any level, the beam remains on the spot until it dissolves. The beam can also show you the events of the past in a new light and throw a ray of light before you that ensures safe passage into the future.

Lovingly,
Mother Time

My dear One,

Do you see how your mind tends to fall into the same old ruts that are so deeply ingrained within your psyche from linear time? Notice the patterns. You wake up feeling depressed. Your mind seeks a cause for it and then settles upon something or someone to blame. It never questions the validity of its assumption.

The truth is that habit—or mechanical thinking—has taken over, and error reigns. The only antidote is truth, which cannot be found in habitual thought. I will give you a hand and lift you to a green hilltop where we can sit for a while and see all those who suffer as you have in the muddy river of continuous participation in the dark and fearful news of your time that does not match your Spirit's will for you.

Here in the warmth of the sunlight, we can feel the rising joy that comes from noticing the wind and trusting deeply in the process of *this* NOW moment.

Lovingly,
Mother Time

My dear One,

In the midst of your repulsion at the greed, the power plays, the excessive violence of your times . . .

Let the Spirit of healing and creating rise within you.

In the midst of your pain over the suffering of individuals, groups, and nations . . .

Let the Spirit of healing and creating rise within you.

In the midst of your concern for those who have lost their soul-spirit connection in a world that has forgotten the sacred . . .

Let the Spirit of healing and creating rise within you.

In the midst of your longing for children and young people to have an opportunity to grow into their natural state of grace . . .

Let the Spirit of healing and creating rise within you.

In the midst of your longing to provide elders with respect for their continuing inner growth . . .

Let the Spirit of healing and creating rise within you.

In the midst of your own loneliness and longing for true spiritual community . . .

Let the Spirit of healing and creating rise within you.

In the midst of your own need to translate a deeper understanding of life into individual and cultural renewal . . .

Let the Spirit of healing and creating rise within you and become visible in joyful and practical life work.

Lovingly,
Mother Time

⸎

My dear One,

You ask how to live amidst the violence of your day. My answer must always be the same: Work on the violence in yourself. Cease the attacks that your conditioned mind makes on your body and soul, and the attacks on others will gradually cease as well. The wounds of your time are deep within the individual *and* within the world. Both must be treated with deep gentleness . . .

Move lightly upon the earth, making no disturbance, leaving no trace behind. Move very gently among others, caring for their wounds as well as your own . . .

Touch the earth gently. Feel the cool bark of the tiny bush beside you. It needs your warmth. Touch your loved ones gently and without any judgment at all. They also need your warmth . . .

Listen deeply to the voices of the earth, the cries, the moans, the whispers of the beech trees, the thousand sleigh-bell sounds of the tree frogs, the unselfconscious melody of the creek waters, the singing of the rocks . . .

Listen deeply to the choices of others, their desires and needs, the longings of their hearts . . .

See the earth gently through eyes that love the dried fallen leaves as much as the new green foliage. Love the maidenhair fern and the tiny acorn in the light and darkness in which they dwell . . .

See all in your life gently, loving their shadows as well as their Light . . .

Speak or sing gently to the earth—a poem, a chant, a sound, a prayer . . .

Speak or sing gently to others—a ballad, a lullaby, a love song . . .

The only antidote to the violence of your times, my dear, is the gentleness of Love.

Lovingly,
Mother Time

My dear One,

You are beginning to understand that the spiritual journey into soul time can lead you to everything you really want for your life— peace, joy, harmony, and love. You see, my child, the old images of humankind are dissolving and can be replaced by a new understanding of the soul's conjunction with Spirit and the natural world.

For this to happen, there must be a breakdown of the old before the birth of the new can take place. This momentous event is taking place simultaneously within the individual and the universe, and you are privileged to be a participant in this great turning. Old thought forms, old habits, old attitudes are being replaced so that a new understanding of soul time based on the interrelatedness between soul-spirit and the natural world can arise on the rubble of the old.

By allowing this transformational process to work within you, you will give others courage to do the same.

Lovingly,
Mother Time

My dear One,

Let me help you see things even more clearly. You are aware that each individual created in the image and likeness of the Creator is likewise a creator. That, in fact, each soul is an artist—an artist of its own life.

Consider each new day and how you weave together a tapestry from the persons, events, and circumstances of your day— pulling one thread from an idea here and another from an event there as you watch the continuity of patterns emerge. Think of days when you choose to take out certain threads or even begin again.

Think about how you paint each new day. What colors do you choose? What brush? Then consider how you sculpt each new day by giving it dimension, shape, and form. Consider also how you sculpt each person you encounter, and how, in turn, they sculpt you.

Each soul is given the raw materials of his or her own life, including the miracle of the body as an instrument of sensing. Seeing, listening, touching, tasting, smelling, all link to the Divine gift of the imagination, which fires creativity. Every child is an example of this miracle as they naturally use their senses to connect to the inner imagination and the outer world. In such a way, the child's soul force is strengthened, and a unique identity is formed that is strong enough to meet the exigencies of their life, provided the child is continuously encouraged to express their life experiences. Through that expression, the child finds integration and meaning. If this process is not encouraged—or is discouraged—the child loses touch with their essential reality as a creator, and that energy, not finding a suitable outlet, can become destructive.

Even if it does not become overtly destructive, the creative process, if not allowed to flourish consciously, will continue within the psyche, buried under layers of time and responsibility, until it can erupt in distressing and illness-producing ways. You see, my dear, the soul is here to create, or should I say, to *re-create,* what it most truly knows, *which is its own direct experience of life.* And that is what it must share, so that the truth of its own direct experience, when put together with the truth of other's direct experience, can create a new kingdom on Earth.

With the absolute uniqueness of the imagination of each soul, each person can make their own contribution to the new perspectives so desperately needed at this time. So for you, who have become disconnected with the creative process, the way back to health and wholeness is through practice.

See all things in their particularity without judgment at the inner or outer level. *Listen* to the sounds around you and within you. Let *smell* and *taste* come into you, and allow yourself to *touch* and be *touched.* From these experiences, the storehouse of the imagination will be reawakened and restocked, and your creativity will flow from it. You will offer up who and what you are.

Do not be discouraged. In the inner life, all are children.

Lovingly,
Mother Time

✒

My dear One,

You have asked me to comment on the idea of leadership as it is trying to evolve in the twenty-first century in which you live.

As humankind recovers the soul-spirit connection, the present diminished idea of leadership based on power and manipulation of one over another will fade, and a new understanding will take its place. This will be based on a model of teaching and learning, giving and receiving. Each individual will become a leader *and* a follower in a world in which greater consciousness of the soul-spirit connection is the aim of all life. Each will know that out of this greater awareness, social problems will be seen and resolved in a new Light, and abundance will follow. Each individual will have the task of keeping the soul-spirit connection alive and will embody that connection.

Individuals, based on the degree of their understanding, will become teacher-guides to whom certain students will be assigned. When the teacher has offered what they know, the student will move on to other teacher-guides. The teacher-guide, in turn, will gravitate to those whose embodiment of the soul-spirit connection is clearer than their own. Teacher-guides will become students, and students will become teacher-guides in a continuous cycle.

All teacher-guides will understand that they dwell within the larger whole of soul time of which they are a part, and that their thoughts, words, and deeds must constantly reflect their memory of the whole. All will know that their own soul-spirit connection must be carefully maintained if they are to create a context for others to remember theirs. This means that they must take responsibility for their own shadow-side, as well as their own innate wisdom and creativity. They must acknowledge the way they *weave* together ideas, people, and materials, the way they *sculpt* one another through their interactions, the way they *color* a moment with their responses. All teacher-guides will know that they have a unique function to perform and will seek to do no less and no more, acknowledging at all times the particularity and originality of others with whom they share a constant teaching and learning community.

The new teacher-guide model will be based not on an individualistic model of power and an egocentric world view, but on an individuality which acknowledges the soul-spirit connectedness within a cosmic world view.

Lovingly,
Mother Time

My dear One,

Today I wish to speak further about the mystery of the spiritual journey into soul time. You have chosen to incarnate at a time in the evolution of humanity when it is seriously out of balance, and you recognize that a good part of your work is to understand how to correct that balance, beginning with your relationship to your own life.

For each soul, everything begins with *one's direct experience.* This is the true definition of faith. Others can help you through their understanding, but you must discover this for yourself. One's primary task is to develop the relationship to one's own soul, mind, and body. The awakened soul must seek first the Spirit from which it has become disconnected, utilizing the mind and body to accomplish this task. It must find its way home to the spiritual realm of soul time from whence it came using the raw materials of its own life to build a bridge, as it were, to a spiritual world that it has never fully forgotten. It has caught glimpses of that world in certain translucent moments, in wisps of songs, in fragments of fragrances, in gentle shuddering touches that cause it to recall an ancient memory in which it was united with that kingdom, that holy dwelling place. Its greatest desire is to rediscover and recover that kingdom.

And so the journey of the awakened soul begins—up from rock and mud and heavy liquid, then water, then air, then light, and then thought. The soul discovers it must take complete responsibility for itself through thought, and that thought must ever be brought into alignment with the thought of the Spirit, which comes from the heart. This thought of Spirit united with the will of the soul has as its aim the highest happiness and Love, not only for the individual soul but for all others whom the soul touches.

One reason so many fail to embark upon the journey of the soul is deep fear of sacrifice and loss. In truth, the spiritual world of soul time longs to give only joy. As a soul increasingly learns to trust and receive this joy, it can then offer it to others, pouring out a healing balm on a world in pain in a gesture of inexpressible gratitude.

Today, practice receiving joy. Look for it as you move your limbs, look up at the sky, measure the moments of connection between you and others as you share gratitude, caring, and love.

Lovingly,
Mother Time

My dear One,

You are now being asked to speak of what you know in relationship to a new imagination of soul-family life, and you have asked me to guide you in this task.

You are being asked to speak in *unfamiliar* ways about the most basic context for nourishing the soul and the outer world, and the relationship between them. In a time of crises and disintegration of family life, you are asked to offer a new picture of holiness-wholeness that must begin with an understanding of each individual as a deeply purposeful, self-unfolding soul created by Love and connected to the vast and mysterious evolving drama of the cosmos.

Throughout the life journey, each soul must come to honor their essential spiritual identity in relationship to the world. The first and most primary context for doing this is within a soul-family unit, which acknowledges itself as one whole and also as part of a larger whole—the meaning of the word "unit." Within the matrix of the soul-family in this picture, the soul is nourished and strengthened and supported inwardly and outwardly by those who understand the sacred tasks entrusted to them.

In this new imagination of the soul-family, some questions that would live within each adult member of the family unit are: What can we give the children? How can we strengthen their unique soul forces? How can we help them find and acknowledge the courage and strength to meet the exigencies of life? How can we help them keep their own innate spirituality alive? How can we nurture their creative imagination in a culture that continually bombards them with images of violence, disease, and alienation? How can we give them faith in the life process? How can we help them discover the Love that lies beneath all doubt, discouragement, disillusionment, grief, and pain? How can we help them trust that the descent into darkness is the ascent into Light? In what ways can we communicate the legacy of forgiveness that has been bequeathed to us through grace? How can we free them from being victimized by their own temperaments? How can we break harmful family patterns from the past? How do we develop within the soul-family unit a sense of community that deeply honors the relationship between teaching and learning among all members—the original meaning of *discipleship?*

Within a soul-family unit in which such questions are *lived,* each generation has specific functions. Parents clearly have the primary responsibilities for daily life and for mediating between the external world and the developing soul needs of their young. They would encourage their young souls to see *with their own eyes* and to express and honor what they see. They would keep the creative imagination alive by helping their children discover images of beauty and joy in their daily lives. They would help them develop critical thinking skills with which to meet the world. They would help them assimilate their life experiences and begin the process of helping them develop values that carry their own convictions. They would help them keep and expand their relationship to the natural world, knowing it to be the primary source of continuing inspiration and renewal for their entire life journey.

Parents in this new imagination of soul-family life would share their own vulnerabilities and struggles within the family unit as a means of demonstrating their trust in the life process. And they would daily model the practice of forgiveness through flexibility and non-judgment. They would also be willing to confront the darkness in themselves and their young and to bring it to Light so that it could be healed by grace.

Grandparents, farther along in the life process, would have different functions within the soul-family unit. They would know that their primary task is to remember the sacredness of all of life and to remember the spiritual essence of each family member, thereby "holding the vision" when others forget or need to rebel as part of their own ongoing development. They would share what they have learned out of their own direct experiences without judgment and without prescription, always recognizing that their own life lessons are also ongoing. Above all else, they would demonstrate the power of love and faith in a future to be created out of Love. They would always remember their place in the succession of life, respecting those souls that preceded them, and loving those who follow with a steadfast love. They would honor all diversity within the knowledge of the constant capacity of Love to steady and calm the pendulum swings of emotions, to infuse the mind with new direction, to motivate the will to act. They would always remember that to serve the life process is to help those who follow to build their own soul-family unit, which must turn outward and become successively wider and more inclusive in order to extend the sense of family beyond bloodlines to others, the natural world, and the universe.

Such an imagination of soul-family life is trying to make itself felt through you to share with others.

Lovingly,
Mother Time

❧

My dear One,

You will pass through zones of negative energy in both your internal world and the external world. These are areas in which you cannot find life because the thought-forms within these zones have lost whatever energy they may have once held for you. It is another way of saying that your values have radically shifted and that you can no longer go back without diminishing your soul-spirit connection in soul time. If you attempt to do so, you will discover that you have lost power and energy and must go deeply within to renew yourself.

There are also physical places on Earth that were once vibrant forms for the consciousness that had evolved to that point. Now that consciousness has expanded to higher levels, these places are simply husks. Spirit has left them to seek forms that consciously receive it. Of these new forms, there are presently very few. Most institutional forms on Earth are hollow, lifeless shells where no inspired thought is possible. The new forms will be created out of the transformed lives of individuals on Earth who are open to the indwelling of Spirit and are willing to move in the direction it leads.

On the internal level, you will be tempted to engage in behaviors that are no longer appropriate for the consciousness that you now carry. When you do so, you will feel as if you have temporarily abandoned your Self. You say, "I let go of the old, but I do not know what will take its place." We sympathize with you, but you have been in such a thicket many times before, and you have always been shown a tiny opening to the next step. Such will be the case again as you continue to trust your own life process.

You say you are dizzy from your own fluctuations. One day, you feel you are on the right track; the next day, you feel lost again. But notice, my dear, the modulations are not as great as they used to be. The pendulum arcs are milder now, and clarity comes more frequently. You will find your way more quickly as you give over and release your life more fully to the Spirit in soul time.

To be willing to walk without knowing in this way is to know.

Lovingly,
Mother Time

My dear One,

You have asked me to speak to you of "direction" and of what "goals" must be set for the inner life. I must tell you that rather than setting "goals" in the linear fashion that characterizes "Passing Time," I will offer you prayers that may assist you and others in finding the Way within soul time:

Divine Spirit . . .

Let our souls be nourished today through the giving and receiving of Love within each encounter. In each of these, let us feel the presence of the Whole . . . the holy . . .

Let us remember to keep our minds clear and empty of all attacks on ourselves or others. Let us not sit on the dark, dank floor in the cave of judgment, but move with unblinking eyes into the Light beyond . . .

Let us be willing to trust our own deepest feelings and truths so that we may always live from the deepest Source within ourselves . . .

Let us be willing to enter into the deep abyss of our own pain and go to the bottom of it in order to find the healing that is always there . . .

May the struggles of this weary century be transformed into the Light of a new day. Release us from our own pain so we may contribute to that transformation . . .

Let us remember that in order for spiritual reality to become visible, we must let go of all judgment and be willing to become transparent . . .

Let us remember that we live within the huge temple of soul time where all may safely enter and abide . . .

Let us keep going past the strident voices and negative racist images in this century and create new worlds of common good for the future . . .

Let us remember that the only true liberation is liberation from the darkness and pain our country has carried for so long. Let it be brought to the Light of soul time and be transformed . . .

Let us remember to be patient and to remember that our personal healing is leading to the healing of the planet. Let the ancient oak tree speak to us of patience and timelessness . . .

Let us learn to honor our own lives—our deep capacity for relationship, our sensitivity to the earth, our appreciation of ritual and the sacred . . .

Let our inner perceptions increase and become spiritual knowledge we can share with others to "grow on" toward the Light . . .

Let our Spirits rise from the heavy shrouds of dogma and ideology and converge as flames with the Spirits of others so we may dance together . . .

Let us freely participate in a time of healing as we release the heavy chains that have bound us to unconscious patterns of mind and heart. Let those chains become golden threads from which we may sew new seamless garments.

Let us daily transform the metallic numbness of this century by our uniquely personal expressions of Love . . .

Let each day reflect the whole of which we are an integral part . . .

Let us be willing to listen to the voices of the world that long to speak to us. Beyond "Past Time," which would pull us backward, and "Passing Time," which would push us forward, let us remember to live *within* soul time where the holiness of *present* moments may be found . . .

And let us find joy within these moments.

Lovingly,
Mother Time

My dear One,

It is almost dark as you continue to grope your way toward the summit of the mountain. Your breathing is labored and your progress slight as you reach a higher altitude where the air is thin . . .

You reach out for a low branch of a slender pine tree, which lends you its momentary support as you struggle for a foothold to stabilize your climb. You look upward to try and guess how much farther you have to go but realize it would be unwise to press on to the summit of the mountain as darkness deepens. You know there is no turning back, so carefully look about you for level ground to spend the night.

I am present here keeping watch over you and directing your attention to a snug little cave just a few yards away that seems to have been abandoned. It has a small ledge around it. Cautiously move toward it and toss your backpack into the cave, then move to rest on the ledge with some food and water as the skies darken and the moon begins to rise.

Despite great fatigue, your mind is anxiously seeking answers to questions of why you are here at this moment in time, why you have risked this dangerous undertaking, and what the meaning might be. Know that I am here as always to try and speak to your concerns as they are common to large numbers of other souls who feel their lives are a difficult climb with great risks of falling.

I needn't remind you that you live in a time of great historic confusion in which strong forces within the universe are at work that must be brought into balance and maintained by reuniting opposites. The darkness of this time on Earth is great, and much Light is required to bring about the desperately needed balance now . . .

You and countless others are trying to understand how to offer the spiritual help necessary to strengthen the Light on Earth, and you have felt compelled to climb this mountain to seek deeper wisdom. You are embracing radical trust in Spirit to make this journey, and although you have fallen back many times, you have always been given a way to continue . . .

In this moment, continue by resting on the ledge and gazing upward to the rising of the full moon and let me share with you a perspective that can perhaps help you understand more fully.

The world, as you have known it, is going through a major transition, as I have told you many times before. The Divine purpose of the creation was meant to be understood as a loving *unity* of physical and spiritual dimensions guided by the Holy Spirit of God, but that sacred purpose was forgotten. Development of the soul-spirit life was neglected with devastating consequences that you are painfully aware of at this time.

You and a large host of others have been awakened to the Original purpose of Love, which can have a healing effect on the whole of creation but requires a willingness to let go of past patterns of thought and to follow an unknown pathway guided by inner Spirit. You have sought to follow that pathway, and your willingness to do so has strengthened you to be here . . . in this moment . . . in the light of a full moon, close to the summit of this mountain.

The moon has special significance for you this night. A full moon means that it is time to release what no longer serves, a time when endings are necessary in order to make room for new wisdom to grow into consciousness. It would be well for you to contemplate in this NOW moment your completion of past patterns and embrace the changes that you are embodying more and more fully as you have awakened to the spiritual truth of your being.

You are letting go of the limited personality self and moving into the larger Self of the heart connected to all living things. As you do, you allow Love to erase all separation and come to fully understand that relationships are the primary context of existence.

The Light within you that cannot be extinguished has entered the darkness of this time. Let go of fear and trust this moment. And sleep well . . .

Lovingly,
Mother Time

∞

My dear One,

Last night you learned that the darkest part of the journey is often before the dawn, and now you are experiencing an entirely new day. Each day can be seen as a new beginning for those who live in the Spirit.

As you now stand at the summit of the mountain in the bright light of the new morning, you look down through the low-lying clouds at the grand vista below to a sight of sheer wonder. There, for miles impossible to gauge, you watch in awe as a multitude of souls in the valley walk slowly up the long, winding road toward the dawning sun . . . truly, a vision of the Family of Humankind walking toward the Light. Stop, breathe slowly, and take this in.

This holy moment touches you deeply and it is why you have been called . . . here . . . to this mountaintop today . . . in soul time . . . to receive this vision of the sacred journey being undertaken by souls all over the world—a journey that has been ongoing since the beginning of time. A journey of soul travelers through the ages seeking the Light of new identity and transformed ways of seeing and being as the very context of their lives.

Now, great numbers of others in this twenty-first century are joining the journey, seeking a new dawning in an expanding universe. They are keenly aware of the evolutionary momentum of their times and are seeking ways of personal and collective change. They long for new understanding of inner experiences of the Divine arising from deep within their own hearts and minds in this time of transition on Earth. They long to find individual purpose in creating a new century away from hatred, disease, and destruction, and they long to move into authentic relationships with others who share the same soul longings.

Your own journey has been long and arduous. You have learned that reconnecting with Spirit each day in soul time offers the possibility of transforming every moment of your life. That same Spirit connects you and every living thing to the Divine in One sacred community. With this understanding, you come to see your journey has been about learning to love the whole of creation. It is a message that MUST be remembered in your time.

Hold yourself in this deep place of Love and retain all faith in your own convictions.

Go now, leave the mountaintop and join the ongoing evolutionary journey moving heart and Spirit forces forward . . . toward the Light.

Lovingly,
Mother Time

ACKNOWLEDGMENTS

PERHAPS THE WORD "RECOGNITION" is more appropriate here because its definition seems more in keeping with soul time: understanding, acceptance, awareness, and realization. This is what I'd like to express to the following people who gave their loving attention and time to this book. Each has offered their special gifts, acceptance, and awareness of the soul journey—a journey we all share as spiritual companions during this time of historic confusion.

First of all, I'd like to recognize my dear soul friend and life partner, Scott Davis, who continually supports all efforts with his considerable talents, skills, and love; Dr. Carole Chase, now transitioned, who resolutely typed the first manuscript despite severe health issues; and Dr. Robert Sardello, distinguished author and founder of Spiritual Psychology, and my beloved daughter-in-law, Janice Toben, who decades ago encouraged the publication of the Mother Time letters.

Special thanks to Pam Brumbaugh, Carol Lenox, Katherine Savage, Karen Delahunty, Daisy Radigan, Mary Southard, Bridget Sperduto, and Carrether Harper for their friendship and invaluable proofreading help in the midst of the perils of the pandemic, and the authors Joyce Rupp, Nan Watkins, Rosemary Ganley, Lina Landess, and Maureen Wild for their generous offerings.

Finally, my everlasting gratitude to the natural world—the creatures, plants, trees, waters, winds, sun, moon, and stars—for providing a holy place for imagination, creativity, Love, Light, soul, and Spirit to flourish.

Suggested Readings

THE FOLLOWING BOOKS and manuscripts have been helpful to me on my journey into soul time. Perhaps they can be of value to you as well . . .

Bachelard, Gaston. *The Poetics of Space*

Belitsos, Byron. *Your Evolving Soul*

Benner, David G., PhD. *Presence and Encounter*

Berry, Thomas. *The Dream of the Earth*

_____. *The Great Work: Our Way Into the Future*

_____. *The Sacred Universe*

Betti, Mario. *The Sophia Mystery in Our Time*

Bruteau, Beatrice. *Evolution Toward Divinity: Teilhard de Chardin and the Hindu Traditions*

Cobb, Edith. *Ecology of the Imagination in Childhood*

Dossey, Larry, M.D. *Recovering the Soul: A Scientific and Spiritual Search*

Duffy, Kathleen, SSJ. *Teilhard's Mysticism: Seeing the Inner Face of Evolution*

Dundas, Alan, Ed. *Sacred Narrative: Readings in the Theory of Myth*

Eakins, Pamela, PhD. *Tarot of the Spirit*

Faricy, Robert, SJ. *The Spirituality of Teilhard de Chardin*

Foundation for Inner Peace. *A Course in Miracles*

Griffiths, Jay. *A Sideways Look at Time*

Helminski, Kabir Edmund. *Living Presence*

Hillman, James. *The Force of Character and the Lasting Life*

_____. *The Soul's Code: In Search of Character and Calling*

Jacobi, Jolande. *The Way of Individuation*

James, Alan. *A Passion for Pilgrimage*

Johnson, Elizabeth A. *Women, Earth, and the Creator Spirit*

Judson, Sylvia Shaw. *The Quiet Eye*

King, Ursula. *Toward a New Mysticism: Teilhard de Chardin and Eastern Religions*

Lewis, C.S. *The Screwtape Letters*

Martin, Calvin Luther. *In the Spirit of the Earth: Rethinking History and Time*

McLeod, Anita. *Elder Wisdom: Searching for Truth in Circles of Women*

Merton, Thomas. *A Book of Hours*

_____. *The Inner Experience: Notes on Contemplation*

Moore, Thomas. *Care of the Soul*

Nepo, Mark. *The Book of Awakening*

_____. *Seven Thousand Ways to Listen*

Newell, J. Philip. *Echo of The Soul: The Sacredness of the Human Body*

Nicoll, Maurice. *Living Time and the Integration of the Life*

_____. *The New Man: An Interpretation of Some Parables and Miracles of Christ*

Ó Murchú, Diarmuid. *Reclaiming Spirituality*

O'Donohue, John, *Eternal Echoes*

_____. *Anam Cara: Book of Celtic Wisdom*

Pierpoint, Katherine. *"Are we nearly there yet?"—The Soul's Longing as Human/Divine, and as Evolutionary Impulse*

Pietener, Carlo. *Transforming Earth, Transforming Self*

Purce, Jill. *The Mystic Spiral: Journey of the Soul*

Rifkin, Jeremy. *Time Wars*

Rohr, Richard. *The Universal Christ*

Rupp, Joyce. *Dear Heart, Come Home*

_____. *Prayer Seeds*

Sardello, Robert. *Facing the World with Soul*

_____. *Love and the Soul: Creating a Future for Earth*

Steiner, Rudolf. *Aspects of Human Evolution*

_____. *The Evolution of Consciousness*

Strong, Mary. *Letters of the Scattered Brotherhood*

Toben, Carolyn W. *Recovering a Sense of the Sacred: Conversations with Thomas Berry*

_____. *Cultivating a Sense of the Sacred: Practices Inspired by Thomas Berry*

Tomberg, Valentin. *Inner Development: Seven Lectures*

Vaughan-Lee, Llewllyn. *The Return of the Feminine and the World Soul*

ABOUT THE AUTHOR

CAROLYN W. TOBEN, M.Ed., is an educator, author, and creator of new social forms with a spiritual dimension that foster cultural renewal. Her background includes degrees from the University of North Carolina Greensboro (Phi Beta Kappa), extensive postgraduate studies in spirituality, world religions, and depth psychology, and teaching in both secondary and college settings with an emphasis on interdisciplinary education. For many years, she served as a seminar leader in the field of teacher renewal at the North Carolina Center for the Advancement of Teaching and the Center for the Advancement of Renewal for Educators in San Francisco.

In 2000, Carolyn co-founded the Center for Education, Imagination, and the Natural World, which offers children and teachers a new understanding of the human-earth relationship. She now serves on the faculty of Timberlake Earth Sanctuary and the Pickard's Mountain Eco-Institute in North Carolina, where she creates programs and retreats for individuals and organizations seeking renewal and reconnection with the natural world.

A grandmother and great-grandmother, Carolyn is the author of *Recovering a Sense of the Sacred: Conversations with Thomas Berry* and *Cultivating a Sense of the Sacred: Practices Inspired By Thomas Berry,* based on her ten-year personal conversations with the renowned priest, author, and cultural historian, Thomas Berry. She is a recipient of the Sacred Universe Award from The Well Spirituality Center.